MURDER!

The Criminal Conspiracy & Coverup Behind the Slaying of Salida's Most Famous Marshal

Plus3 Press
Denver, CO

Plus3 Press
Denver, CO

To Learn About More Books in this Series, Visit:
www.SalidaWalkingTours.com/shop

For Rez

PLUS3 PRESS BOOKS BY STEVEN T. CHAPMAN

NONFICTION

MURDER! The Criminal Conspiracy & Coverup Behind the Slaying of Salida's Most Famous Marshal (A Salida Walking Tours Historical Biography)

Blood, Booze & Whores: The History of Salida, Colorado, Volume 1—1880 & 1881 (A 'Salida Sam' Historical Book)

Dead Bodies & Brothels: The History of Salida, Colorado, Volume 2—1882 & 1883 (A 'Salida Sam' Historical Book)

Three Murdered Wives: The History of Salida, Colorado, Volume 3—1884 & 1885 (A 'Salida Sam' Historical Book)

Salida Burns Down: The History of Salida, Colorado, Volume 4— 1886 & 1887 (A 'Salida Sam' Historical Book)

Things to Do in Salida—52 Memorable Activities & 104 Souvenir Photographs

Break the Chains! How to Make Money Online, Work from Home & Profit While You Sleep

Home Watch: The Definitive Guide to Starting, Growing and Succeeding in the Vacation Home Care Industry

FICTION

In Eddy We Trust

I Believe in You: Discussions with the Divine

TABLE OF CONTENTS

FROM THE AUTHOR

The saga of Baxter Stingley was one of the first stories I came across in 2018 when investigating the history of Salida, Colorado, for my new business, Salida Walking Tours (www.SalidaWalkingTours.com). The tale sounded incredible and almost too good to be true, involving a fearless, no-nonsense, dedicated public servant who died in the line of duty. The accepted narrative was a man devoted to good, who removed crime from the city and did not tolerate the wild and violent behaviors typical in newly established frontier towns.

Over the next few years, as I read every edition of the regional newspapers from 1880 to 1900, seemingly disconnected stories began creating a more complicated picture of Baxter Stingley. He was undoubtedly brave, a solid lawman committed to bringing order to a boomtown filled with bloodshed and chaos. But a pattern emerged, with Stingley being complicit in questionable activity or, at a minimum, turning a blind eye where friends and family were concerned. Stingley also did not hesitate to use his badge to intimidate opponents.

Marshal Stingley's story is emblematic of the wild west days. Both politicians and police officers regularly leveraged their positions to advance specific causes and to gain wealth. If my conclusions are correct about his behavior and motivations, Baxter Stingley was a typical man of his time, a conflicted and flawed person who probably did more good than harm.

What fascinated me most was connecting a series of dots that indicated Stingley's murder was almost certainly not the result of a random occurrence with a wandering cowboy. Facts point to powerful enemies setting up the Marshal and protecting his killer, then arranging things to ensure justice would never occur.

Murder conspiracies and coverups are by nature convoluted. In these pages, you'll walk with me into the past, examining the methods, motivations, and opportunities of multiple leading citizens in Chaffee, Park, and Fremont Counties. By the end, I'm confident you'll agree that Baxter's Stingley's death, and the escape of his killer, was probably planned and not accidental.

A joy for hardcore history researchers is finding that one obscure bit of information untangling a logic knot and allowing pieces to fall into the proper order. The key to solving Baxter Stingley's murder was creating a list of suspects and players. But that was problematic from the start.

One person key to Baxter's story was Jesse H. Stingley, his brother. Unraveling his story was difficult because of the existence of three Jesse's in Baxter's immediate family. The name was common in the Stingley lineage because of the patriarch, Jesse Bush Stingley. Jesse Bush was father to nine children by his first wife, two by his second, and adoptive father to three. It was the adopted children that ultimately held the keys to determining who was who.

Jesse H. Stingley lived in Salida with his brother, Baxter. Another Jesse H. Stingley later resided in Colorado, and there was a third brother, Martin Jesse Stingley (referred to as Jesse in the United States Census). Many publicly created records, such as those found on ancestry websites, incorrectly intermingled these three men, making a mess and endless confusion.

I 'think' I've figured it out.

Martin Jesse Stingley, born in 1859, seems to have no record after showing up on the 1860 and 1870 United States Census. He vanished, not an uncommon occurrence in that era.

Jesse Huffman Stingley, born in 1869, was the son of Baxter's brother, Absalom. Jesse Huffman arrived in Colorado nearly a decade after his two older cousins and died tragically (*refer to Chapter Thirteen*).

Jesse Hooper, born around 1857, was the missing Stingley, the one who confounded me and other researchers and genealogists.

Two years after the death of his wife, Jesse Bush Stingley wed Susanna Boicourt in 1870. Susanna, the widow of William Hughes, had three children, John (17), Julia (15), and Jesse Hooper (13).

Although I could not find a record, it seems logical that Jesse

Bush Stingley adopted the three, creating another Jesse H. Stingley who was a brother to Baxter.

One ancestry entry lists Jesse as a female, but the census report indicates that this name referred to a male working on the family farm. I trust government records more than unverified submissions on a website. Nothing else adequately explains the score of legal forms, census reports, marriage certificates, and newspaper articles documenting Jesse H. Stingley living in Salida, Colorado beginning November 1881. It certainly could not logically refer to Martin Jesse. Nor could Jesse Huffman be the one—the age, timelines, and spouses do not match.

A frustration of historical investigations is never having absolute certainty. I could be wrong about the identity of Jesse H. Stingley in Salida and the reality behind the killing of his brother, Baxter. But after hundreds of hours of wading through countless files, I believe the research is convincing and correct. I think you'll agree that facts point to Marshal Stingley's murder as a conspiracy, with many influential, well-connected citizens involved in the killing and the resulting coverup.

An endless source of irritation for me when reading nonfiction is footnotes. I hate them. This book, rather than noting a source the reader will likely never research, includes actual newspaper articles, maps, and photographs. Seeing the original accounts allows you to determine if my speculations and thoughts are valid based on the primary statements. Think of it as a written documentary.

I hope you enjoy reading about Benjamin R. Baxter Stingley as much as I reveled in the investigation.

~ Steve Chapman

1870 United States Federal Census for Jessee Stingley

Kansas > Franklin > Ohio

—	Orru	3	f	b	At Home		Ohio		
—	Harriett	4	f	b			Kansas		
30 1/4 1/2	Stingley Jessee	33	m	b	Farmer	600	Kansas	Sep	1
	Susanna	40	f	b	Keping house		Ohio		
—	Rachel	16	f	b	At Home		Indiana		
—	Martha	18	f	b	At Home		Indiana		
—	Jessee	11	m	b			Missouri		
—	Octavia	8	f	b	At Home		Missouri		
—	Ella May	12	f	b			Iowa		
—	Hughes Jared	17	m	b	Farmer		Kansas		
—	Jessee	18	m	b	Farmer		Illinois		
—	Julia	16	f	b	At Home		Illinois		
115 113	Smith Elmore	38	m	b	Farmer	1400 1600	Ohio		1

Occupation

No. of dwellings, 9   No. of white females, 17   No. of union, foreign born, —

" families, 9   " " colored males, 1   " " female, 1

" white males, 21   " " females, —   " " blind,

No. of insane, —

1870 United States Census showing Jesse Huges living with his mother, Susanna, along with Jesee Bush Stingley

CHAPTER ONE

Benjamin R. 'Baxter' Stingley: The Early Years

Baxter Stingley's Childhood

In 1850, he lived with his family in Lauramie, Indiana (age 4).

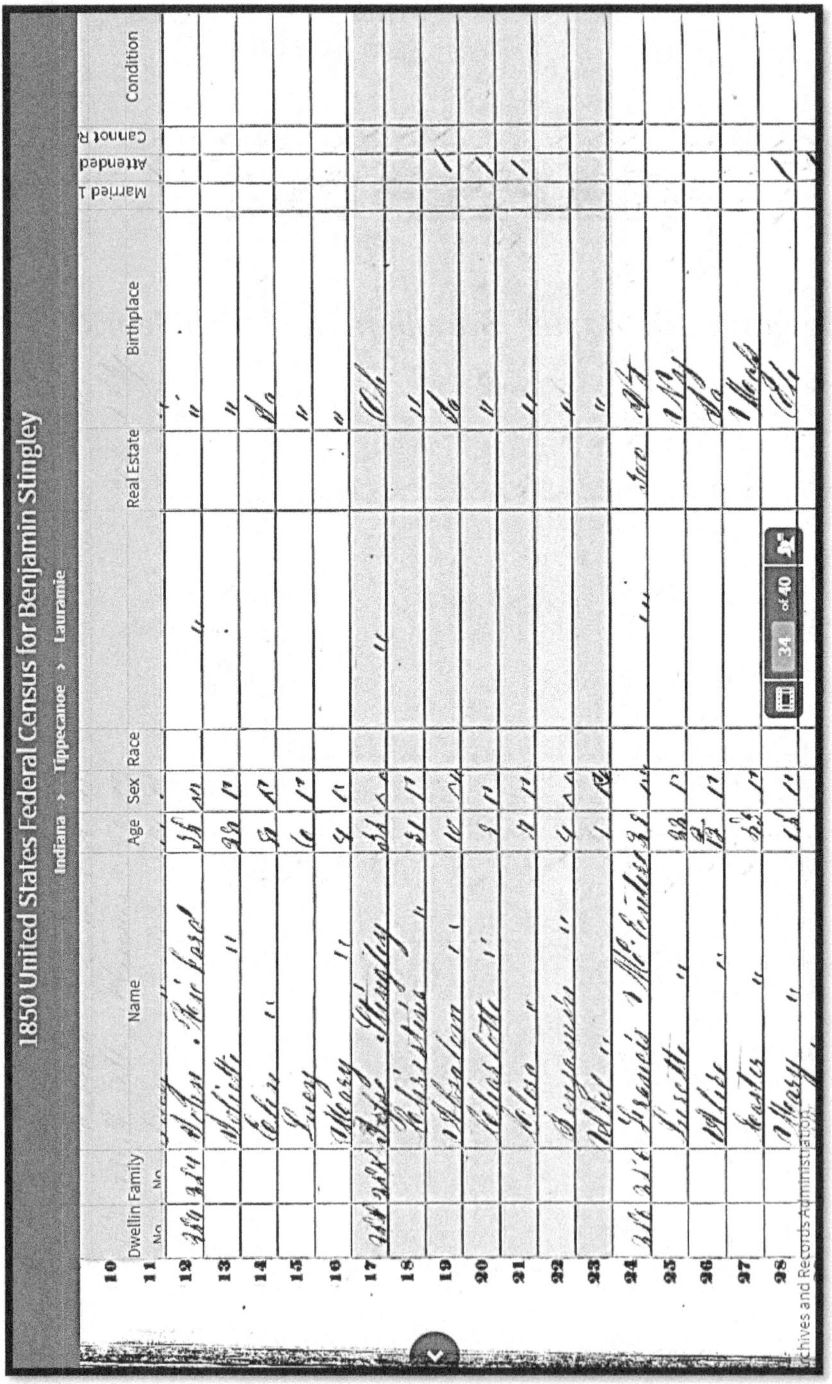
1850 United States Federal Census for Benjamin Stingley
Indiana > Tippecanoe > Lauramie
Dwellin No
Family No
Name
Age
Sex
Race
Real Estate
Birthplace
Married
Attended
Cannot R
Condition
34 of 40

1850 United States Census

In 1860, he lived with his family in Nodaway, Missouri (age 14).

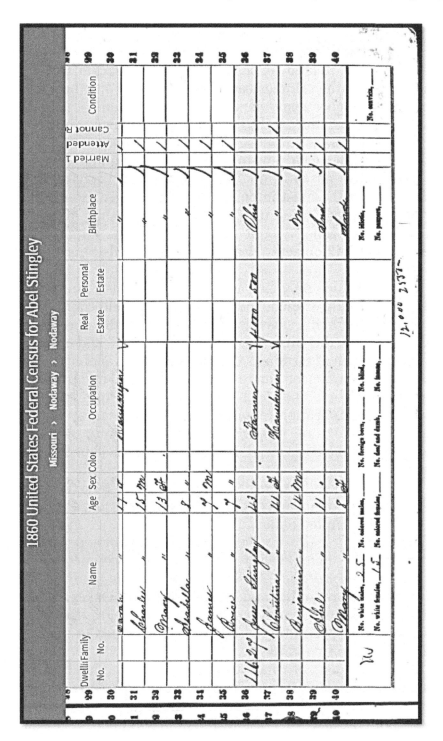

1860 United States Census

Arrival in Colorado

There is no written record of the activities or location of Benjamin R. Baxter Stingley between 1860 and July 1, 1872. On that date, he filed a claim for a 160-acre homestead in Denver, Colorado, under the Homestead Act. Based on the Act's requirements, Stingley would have arrived in Colorado at least by 1867, at the age of 22, during the early days of Denver's boom.

President Abraham Lincoln signed The Homestead Act on May 30, 1862, allowing citizens to own public domain land free of charge (other than an $18 filing fee—around $500 today). It is considered one of the most important pieces of legislation in the history of the United States, turning over vast amounts of public land to private citizens. About ten percent of the nation, two hundred seventy million acres, was claimed and settled under this Act.

A homesteader only had to be the head of a household (meaning men, single women, and former slaves could claim land) and at least 21 years old. Parcels were 160 acres. Requirements included living on the property, building a home, and making improvements, such as farming. After locating an available parcel, there was a five-year period where homesteaders had to 'prove up,' meaning build a home and meet the requirements necessary for ownership. The application required two witnesses agreeing that the land had undergone proper enhancements. After fulfilling these obligations, the homesteader received a patent signed by the President.

The Homestead Act was repealed in 1976, except for in Alaska, where it continued until 1986. Today, there is no possibility of free land in the United States.

Denver was a logical choice for Stingley, a young, poor man from Missouri. The 'Pikes Peak or Bust' movement was encouraged by the book, *History of the Gold Discoveries on the South Platte River,* written by early settler and prospector Daniel Oakes. Oakes distributed thousands of copies throughout Missouri—the book was an instant hit, prompting hundreds of thousands to migrate into Colorado beginning in 1858.

No record exists of what Stingley did with the land. After receiving his land patent, he only stayed in the Denver area a short period before following the gold rush into the mountains of central Colorado. With the discovery of gold at California Gulch, near what is today Leadville, over 10,000 men quickly flowed into the region. Most likely, Stingley sold the Denver parcel, which funded his move to the mountains and helped him start a saloon in the boomtown of Alpine.

32

recd.

The United States of America,

To all to whom these presents shall come, Greeting:

Whereas, In pursuance of the Act of Congress, approved July 2, 1862, entitled "An Act donating Public Lands to the several States and Territories which may provide Colleges for the benefit of Agriculture and the Mechanic Arts," there has been deposited in the General Land Office Scrip No. 738 , for one quarter section of Land, in favor of the State of *Alabama* , duly assigned by the proper authority of the said State to *Benjamin R. B. Stingley*

with evidence that the same has been located upon *the North East quarter of Section Twenty in Township Six South of Range Sixty eight West in the District of Lands subject to sale at Denver Colorado Territory containing One Hundred and Sixty acres*

according to the Official Plat of the Survey of the said Land, returned to the General Land Office by the Surveyor General.

Now know ye, That there is, therefore, granted by the United States unto the said *Benjamin R. B. Stingley as assignee as aforesaid and to his heirs* the tract of Land above described: **To have and to hold** the said tract of Land, with the appurtenances thereof, unto the said *Benjamin R. B. Stingley as assignee as aforesaid* and to his heirs and assigns forever; subject to any vested and accrued water rights for mining, agricultural, manufacturing, or other purposes, and rights to ditches and reservoirs used in connection with such water rights as may be recognized and acknowledged by the local customs, laws, and decisions of courts, and also subject to the right of the proprietor of a vein or lode to extract and remove his ore therefrom, should the same be found to penetrate or intersect the premises hereby granted, as provided by law.

In testimony whereof, I, *Ulysses S. Grant* , President of the United States of America, have caused these letters to be made Patent, and the Seal of the General Land Office to be hereunto affixed.

[L.S.]

Given under my hand, at the City of Washington, the *First* day of *July* , in the year of our Lord one thousand eight hundred and *Seventy two* , and of the Independence of the United States the *Ninety Sixth* .

BY THE PRESIDENT *U. S. Grant*

By *_____* , Secretary.

_____ , Recorder of the General Land Office.

Benjamin R. Baxter Stingley's land patent in Denver, Colorado.
Signed in July 1, 1872.

Alpine to Cleora

According to the United States Census, Stingley lived in Alpine in 1880, one of many mining communities that sprang up in the central Colorado mountains. When he arrived in Alpine is not recorded, but he would have been there at least by 1875 based on his participation in the Lake County War. He left Alpine in the early part of 1880 to seek riches in the new railroad community of Cleora, located along the Arkansas River near present-day Salida.

Cleora sprang up when the Atchison, Topeka, and Santa Fe Railroad picked the location for a new depot for their expanding railroad system. William Bale owned the land. He was one of the original settlers in the Arkansas Valley and operated a stagecoach station before the railroad announced the area as the spot of a new station. After the railroad proclaimed their plans, Bale named the region Cleora, in honor of his youngest daughter, and around 600 people flocked to the new settlement, hoping to make their fortune.

When the Atchison, Topeka, and Santa Fe Railroad lost a protracted legal battle with the Denver and Rio Grande Railroad for rights to the territory, Cleora soon became a ghost town. The Denver and Rio Grande wanted to build their depot where the land was undeveloped (meaning inexpensive) and chose a different site several miles away—a barren, dusty place now known as Salida.

Baxter Stingley, date unknown

1880 United States Federal Census for B. Stingley

Colorado > Chaffee > Alpine > 027

Family No	Name	Race	Sex	Age	Relationship	Single	Married	Widow/Divorced	Occupation	Months U.	Sick	Birthplace	Birthplace of Father	Birthplace of Mother
52/53	Wolfe, Emil	W	M	17		/			Hand Printer			Germany		Ind. Ind.
53/53	O'Neil, R.	W	M	31		/			Printer	2		Ill.	Ireland	Ky.
54/54	Greenman, A.	W	M	22		/			Grocer in Flour Co.			Me.	Me.	Me.
55/55	Brown, M.A.	W	M	49		/			Capt. In Light Mine			Me.		
56/56	Hartman, A.	W	M	50		/			Rack Capt. in Flour			Pa.	Germany	Germany
57/57	Gleason, R.	W	M	39			/		Carpenter			Irg.	Irg.	N.Y.
57/57	Gleason, P.	W	M	41			/		Proprietor			Irg.	Germany	Germany
59/59	Grant, J.C.	W	M	37			/		Stock Dealer			Ill.	Ill.	Ill.
60/60	Franklin, J.	W	M	64	grandson		/		Cattle Dealer			Texas		
60/60	Constantino, Mrs.	W	M	53			/	/	Capt. Broker			Ind.	Cal.	Cal.
61/61	Bailey, A.	W	M	31			/		Carpenter			Ireland	Ireland	Ireland
61/62	Stingley, B.	W	M	34			/		Saloon			Mo.	Ohio	Ohio

United States Census, 1880. Baxter Stingley living in Alpine, Colorado, working as a saloon keeper.

Participation in the Lake County War

When he was 30, Stingley took part in the Lake County War, a multi-year fight typical of the frontier days—a bloody struggle over water and land and grazing rights. Such 'wars' occurred in many western areas.

This conflict officially started in 1875, in what was then Lake County, Colorado, now known as Chaffee County. It was a struggle between newcomers and long-time locals, and the years-long battle exposed the lengths to which ranchers would go to protect their land and ensure they would write the future.

Among the atrocities committed in this conflict was the murder of a sitting judge, a crime historians refer to as one of the most vicious in the annals of history.

Whether you called these men vigilantes or heroes probably depended on which side of the gun you were on. Stingley and his crew murdered several men and forced many others off their homestead claims. Then, most of the gang turned into solid citizens that history refers to as founders and pioneers of the territory.

Triggering the conflict was an incident with a newly arrived farmer named Elijah Gibbs. Gibbs settled in Centerville in 1866. Over the years, Gibbs and his family developed a positive reputation in the community. But as was typical of the era, rumors began circulating that Gibbs, his brothers, and other newcomers started a criminal operation to steal cattle, jump mining claims, and take over properties by any means necessary. Their enemies labeled this group *The Regulators*. Little proof exists about this group's actual existence, but people regularly chose sides in the pioneer days, usually between those new to an area and those who arrived first.

Before Colorado became a State, settlers regularly created laws at the end of a gun. Courts were slipshod at best, corrupt at worst, and alliances often outweighed written rules.

On June 16, 1874, Elijah Gibbs and his hired hand, Stewart McClish, got into an argument with a neighboring rancher named George Harrington. The disagreement was over fencing and water rights. Words turned into punches, and Gibbs pulled a gun to stop the fight from escalating. He claimed the gun went off accidentally, but no one got shot, and neither man received a severe injury.

The following night, Harrington looked out his window and saw one of his outbuildings on fire. Along with his wife, Harrington rushed to the structure with water. Harrington's younger sister watched from the house as she held the couple's infant daughter. While attempting to douse the flames, gunshots rang out from the dark, and, instantly, George Harrington was dead. No one saw the killer.

Because of their earlier fight, Elijah Gibbs and Stewart McClish were immediately labeled suspects and arrested on the charge of murder.

Citizens in the wild west days did not have much faith in legal proceedings, and many of the ranchers wanted to lynch the pair right away. But cooler heads won out, and the Sheriff took Gibbs and McClish to the jail in the nearby town of Granite, the county seat. Poorly constructed calabooses rarely stopped an angry mob, and it became evident to the Sheriff that he would be unable to guarantee the safety of his prisoners, so he transported them to Denver. The hope was that an impartial jury would hear the matter and render a fair verdict.

The Denver jury took five days to hear the case before ruling that Gibbs and McClish were innocent, as no eyewitnesses or evidence placed either man at the scene of the murder.

Stewart McClish had enough and immediately left the Colorado territory, but Elijah Gibbs returned to his homestead.

Things in the community appeared calm after the trial, but it was only a surface illusion. Underneath the public niceties, tensions were brewing, and friends of George Harrington were angry and wanted revenge.

Seven months later, on January 22, 1875, George Harrington's friends obtained a warrant to arrest Elijah Gibbs for assault. Since he was declared innocent of murder, an assault charge was the best they could get, and that was enough to provide the excuse to go after the man.

Sherriff Weldon led a group to Gibbs' ranch one evening to serve the warrant. Most of the men had been drinking heavily, and their intentions were for murder, not justice. Riding up on the ranch, the mob called out for Gibbs to exit his home and take his hanging like a man. Inside the cabin were Elijah Gibbs, his pregnant wife, their three children (under the age of five), and a neighbor lady and her child.

Gibbs knew that if he left the safety of his home, he was a dead man, so he remained inside. The mob decided to burn out Gibbs and piled brush and wood around the house, but recent wet weather soaked the logs, and they would not ignite. Frustrated, the horde rushed the door to break in and capture Gibbs. This conflict was now a life-and-death matter, and Gibbs fired his pistol through the chinks in the wooden walls and his door, killing two of the would-be lynchers.

During the melee, the mob accidentally killed one of their own with a shotgun blast. Seeing that the surprise attack had turned into an unexpected slaughter, the group backed off and left the Gibbs ranch.

The next day, Gibbs turned himself over to the Justice of the Peace in the nearby community of Brown's Creek. The Justice ruled that Gibbs fired in self-defense. But the law was not going to satisfy those who wanted Gibbs dead, and Gibbs knew this truth. Hoping for safety, he rode hard toward Denver, chased the entire way by the vigilantes who nearly captured him in the town of South Park. Sheriff Weldon also pursued Gibbs, determined to arrest the man on the false charge and return him to Lake County, presumably for trial, but most likely to be lynched. Gibbs eluded the lawman and the gang.

Gibbs, his family, and his in-laws never returned to Lake County.

Despite driving Gibbs out of the county, the battle had only begun. Enemies of Gibbs organized, calling their group the *Committee of Safety*. The *Committee of Safety* was composed of the most prominent men in the area, led by a well-known merchant and rancher name Charles Nachtrieb. William Bale, who later started the town of Cleora, and Joseph Hutchinson, one of the first to settle in the valley, were also part of the *Committee of Safety* leadership. So was Baxter Stingley.

The bottom line to all this is that the old-timers worried newcomers would compete for water, land rights, and resources. Keep in mind that Colorado was not a State just yet. Land rights were sketchy, at best.

The group's goal was to rid the county of anyone who supported Elijah Gibbs or called him a friend. The long-brewing animosity between the newcomers and the early settlers had finally turned into an armed dispute.

What no one could foresee was that this fight would last for seven years.

The *Committee of Safety* worked as a combination vigilante group and extralegal judicial body. They ruled the county through violence and intimidation, holding make-shift 'trials,' torturing numerous men, and committing countless murders.

The Territorial Governor attempted to end the dispute by sending a detective into the county, but neither the funds nor the manpower existed to enforce government will.

Among those Stingley and his gang pushed off their land was Ernest Christison. Remember that name because Christison pops up throughout Stingley's story, not always in a positive way.

CHAPTER TWO

May 1880
Out of the Dust Comes a Boomtown

Salida, Colorado, 1883
Courtesy, Salida Regional Library, Salida Centennial Photo Collection

The Birth of Salida, Colorado

Before May of 1880, the area now known as Salida was nothing more than a sage desert—flat, dusty, barren of trees or grass or many people.

Salida was born following the Royal Gorge War (a lengthy legal battle between the Denver and Rio Grande Railroad and the Atchison, Topeka, and Santa Fe Railroad). Lawsuits were filed between the competing companies to determine who had the legal right to build along the Arkansas River.

The competing company planned to build a depot at Cleora, but after winning the lawsuit, the Denver and Rio Grande abandoned that site, located several miles east of Salida. Instead, the Denver and Rio Grande chose a sandy patch of land along the Arkansas River.

Almost immediately, citizens abandoned Cleora—without the railroad, the town had no reason to exist. Within a year, nearly all the 600 citizens relocated. Many migrated to what was then called South Arkansas, later renamed Salida.

The migrants transported entire buildings to the new town, and most businesses moved, including the newspaper, dry goods stores, grocers, and saloon operators such as Baxter Stingley.

The first Denver and Rio Grande Railroad train arrived at the end of May 1880. On June 5, the newspaper, *The Mountain Mail*, printed its first edition. A new town sprang from the dust.

For a detailed history of the founding and growth of Salida, Colorado, read the 'Salida Sam' historical book series. Each edition covers two years in Salida history and contains nearly every factual happening, original photographs, maps, and a searchable index. You can order the books at www.SalidaWalkingTours.com/shop.

CHAPTER THREE

June 1880
Baxter Stingley Arrives in Salida, Colorado

Arrival in Salida

Baxter Stingley was one of the first to arrive in the new boomtown, relocating from Cleora at 35. He immediately started construction on a home located along Second Street near F Street.

Baxter never married, and he had no children, but his brother, Jesse Hooper, eleven years younger, followed Baxter to Salida in November 1881.

Stingley continually searched for success. In Alpine and Cleora, he operated a saloon. In Salida, he did the same, teaming with Charlie Hawkins to open Stingley and Company.

His new saloon, one of the dozens that sprang up almost immediately, was well received by the locals and supported by the newspaper editor.

> Stingley can mix drinks for you in the highest style of the art.

The Mountain Mail, December 4, 1880

> Stingley & Co's is the place to go for a social game of billiards or pool and the best brands of liquors and cigars.

The Mountain Mail, December 11, 1880

Involvement with Government

Baxter Stingley participated in the establishment of government and had eyes set on higher political office. In October 1880, he got appointed to the 'challenging committee.' Their job was to watch the polls for illegal voters in the first elections. Criminals, not wanting the settlement to become officially incorporated, stacked voting lines with out-of-town men sympathetic to their cause (meaning bought and paid for). Boomtowns typically required a period of residency to vote.

> The meeting appointed a committee of five, consisting of A. T. Ryan, W. W. Roller, A. T. Blachly, B. Stingley and M. R. Moore, and named it the challenging committee, whose duty it will be to watch the polls and challenge all suspected illegal voters.

The Mountain Mail, October 23, 1880

Leaving Salida

From May to October of 1880, Salida had no legal status and no law enforcement. Fights were too numerous to count, and armed robberies were common. After a successful vote to incorporate as an official city, the town council appointed the first Marshal, a bartender named James Meadows.

Although the town had less than 300 citizens, Marshal Meadows had a difficult job, attempting to control men who were rugged and used to making their own rules. During his second week on the job, Meadows received a neck wound when ambushed by a man he arrested earlier in the day. Following the shooting of Marshal James Meadows (he recovered in two weeks), Baxter got appointed as temporary Marshal.

In December, Stingley followed his life pattern—he saw more significant opportunity in the next 'can't miss boomtown' and sold his interest in the saloon to his partner, Charlie A. Hawkins. Stingley then traveled a few miles upriver to the new city of Poncha Springs, where he opened another bar.

C. A. Hawkins has purchased Baxter Stingley's interest in their billiard hall and will run it alone in future. Stingley goes to Poncha along with the boom to run a saloon

The Mountain Mail, December 18, 1880

PON   257   PON

Brunfield, M., restaurant and photographer.
Carstarphen, Geo. B., notary public.
Carstarphen & Co., lumber, hardware, furniture, etc.
Cherry, Huston & Co., gen'l mdse.
Chisholm, James, blacksmith.
Clute, R. J., saddlery.
Collins, D. W., physician.
Collins & Fowler, physicians.
Cottage Home Hotel, Mrs. E. E. Moore, propr.
Craig, L. W., dry goods, clothing, etc.
Cruzen, G. W., painter.
Derr, J. J. & Co., drugs, stationery.
Derr, Misses, dressmakers.
Derr, Phillip, millinery.
Devereaux, R. & Co., saloon.
Doyle & Hunter, livery and sale.
Fletcher, R. E., groceries, bakery and restaurant.
Florida. Forbes & Co., forwarding and commission.
Forrinkel, J. H., shoemaker.
Fulton, H. H., post master and books and stationary.
Furst, Jos., baker and barber.
Garrison, B. F., attorney.
Hale, G. F. restaurant.
Howell, F. D., jewelry.
Hurdle, T. J., restaurant.
Hyers & Abiet, gen'l mdse.
Jackson, H. A., livery, feed and sale.
Johnson, Mrs , dressmaker.
Knight, J. C., station agt.
Lindsay, A., furniture.
Mack, A B., hardware.

Mack, Henry, lumber.
McGlaughlin & Turner, grocer's.
McKelvey, W. L., blacksmith.
Meyer, Dale & Co , groceries and provisions.
Meyers & Albright, gen'l mdse.
Mickey, J. T., manager smelter.
Mix, M., boarding house and restaurant.
Mullen & Barret, saloon.
Murray, Lewis, meat market.
Neeley Mining and Smelting Co., Brett, manager.
Nichols, Robert, saloon.
Patterson, J. H., carpenter.
Pender & Laub, wh'sale liquors.
Poncha Springs daily Herald, W. C. & W. F. Tompkins, props.
Poncha Springs Free Library.
Poncha Springs Hotel, Asbury & Gray, props.
Poncha Springs Town Company.
Powers, James E., music hall and restaurant.
Quaintance Hotel, S. D. Quaintance, prop.
Rigby, Chas. W., restaurant.
Rossa, Joseph, shoemaker.
Russell & McCaldy, backsmiths.
Sanderson & Co.'s daily stages to Gunnison City and Bonanza.
Smith, G. H., blacksmith.
Sprague & Redcliff, meat market.
Steele, G. W., gen'l mdse.
Stingley, Baxter, saloon.
Stingley & Co., wh'sale liquors.
Stuart, W. J., stage agent.
Telfer, Miller & Co., lodging house and painters.
Thomas, A. J., lumber and hardware.

City Directory, 1881

DISSOLUTION OF CO-PARTNERSHIP.

Notice is hereby given that the co-partnership heretofore existing between Baxter Stingley and C. A. Hawkins, under the firm name of Stingley & Co., is this day dissolved by mutual consent. All accounts against the firm will be paid by C. A. Hawkins.

BAXTER STINGLEY   C. A. HAWKINS.

Salida, Colorado, January 1, 1881.

The Mountain Mail, December 18, 1880

Return to Salida

Stingley's infatuation with Poncha Springs lasted until the following Spring. He returned to Salida in May 1881 but bounced in and out of town for the next five months, chasing fame and fortune in each new boomtown that popped up throughout the high country. *The Mountain Mail* tracked most comings and goings, easy to do when the total city population is only 300 and recorded Stingley's travels.

> Baxter Stingley dropped in to see us Friday morning. He reports Junction City improving rapidly.

The Mountain Mail, August 27, 1881

CHAPTER FOUR

August 13, 1881
Violent Cowboys & First Signs of Trouble

A Rowdy Night

Salida, Colorado was as wild as any town in the old west—it just did not receive the press coverage of better-known places.

Before Baxter Stingley became Marshal, an incident occurred epitomizing the violence and unpredictability of the new settlement. This story also introduces characters who will later become part of Baxter's legacy.

On a Saturday evening, August 13, 1881, young cowboys rode with bad intentions into town. The men were Ernest Christison, Roe Cameron, Billy Taylor, and Edwin Watkins.

Soon after arriving, they began shouting and shooting guns into the air, terrifying local citizens and sending men scattering for cover. Some of the group wandered to the bridge and held up a couple walking near the upper bridge.

Just after dark, Roe Cameron searched for Ernest Christison as the men became separated during their rowdiness. Cameron walked into several saloons and businesses, his revolver drawn and pointed, shouting he would "shoot the damn son-of-a-bitch (Christison) if he could find him."

Cameron walked into Matt Heizer's butcher shop and fired his gun. Then, he held Heizer at gunpoint and repeatedly snapped his weapon in the man's face, terrifying the shop owner.

The town Marshal hid during the melee, which allowed the cowboys to run wild for several hours. Only the bravery of Deputy Sheriff Al Ryan, and a few local men, stopped the cowboys, or someone would undoubtedly have died. Ryan tossed the drunken Cameron into the jail. The next day, a Sunday, Judge William Hawkins released Roe Cameron on bail. On Monday, Cameron pleaded guilty in court and received a fine of $50 (around $1,000 in modern worth).

Because of his cowardice and refusal to act, the town council fired the Marshal.

Last Saturday afternoon and evening a crowd of the cow boys from above came to town for a good time. They had it. In the crowd were Roe Cameron, Billey Taylor, Earnest Christison, Watkins and another man. Some of them got a little too full for their own safety and the comfort of those with whom they came in contact. They indulged in the game of firing off their revolvers, and also went so far as to hold up a man who with his wife was out walking near the upper bridge. Just after dark awhile Cameron, who was looking for Christison, from who he had been separated, walked into several places with a drawn revolver, swearing he would "shoot the damned son-of-a-bitch" if he could find him. He went into Heizer's butcher shop and discharged his revolver once, and then covered Matt and began snapping the revolver in his face. While he was engaged in this little amusement deputy sheriff Ryan collared him and with the assistance of other parties carried him off to the calaboose. The next day, Sunday, he was released on bail, and on Monday went before Justice Hawkins, plead guilty to charges pending against him and was fined fifty dollars.

The Mountain Mail, August 20, 1881

First Signs of Future Trouble

Piecing together the specifics of a criminal conspiracy requires imagining beyond the obvious.

The night of August 13, 1881, might have involved nothing more than drunken young men flexing their muscles. Cameron, Watkins, Taylor, and Christison were in their early- to late-twenties. In any period, men of that age often act irresponsibly, often dangerously, especially when drinking.

Worth particular notice are the actions of Roe Cameron. The man he terrorized with his gun, Matt Heizer, was the business partner of Roe's father, Thomas. Heizer opened a meat market the first week of May 1881. Several weeks later, Heizer added Thomas Cameron as a partner.

> Matt Heizer will open a wholesale and retail meat market in a few days in the building second door south of Mulvany's store. Mr. Heizer is an old hand at the business and will undoubtedly keep a good stock of meats. When he opens next week give him a call.

The Mountain Mail, May 7, 1881

A good detective must first conceive possibilities, often drawn from circumstantial evidence. As shown in *Chapter Eight*, Thomas Cameron, Ernest Christison, Edwin Watkins, Jesse Stingley, and others were part of a large cattle theft ring.

Heizer may have taken on Thomas Cameron as a partner for financial reasons, but it is reasonable to assume Cameron offered something extra to the partnership—access to inexpensive cattle.

Cameron & Heizer,
MEAT MARKET.

WHOLESALE AND RETAIL
AT
THE LOWEST MARKET PRICE.

On First street, where a good supply of fresh Beef, Pork, Veal, Mutton, Etc., will always be found, both for the WHOLESALE AND RETAIL trade.

They will also keep a full line of

VEGETABLES.

GIVE THEM A CALL.

Salida,   -   -   Colorado.

The Mountain Mail, May 21, 1881

Thomas Cameron's ranch neighbor was Edwin Watkins. They both lived in Adobe Park, just outside of Salida.

Watkins and Christison's involvement in cow theft is undeniable, as shown later, but each probably had different roles. On several occasions, Christison got caught red-handed, moving stolen beef. Watkins never was proven to have directly stolen anything, but his ranch was a known hiding place for the cows. For several years, ranchers could not figure out how small numbers of their herd, 60-70 at a time, disappeared without any trace.

The most likely scenario is that the cattle were quickly butchered, either on Watkins's ranch or that of his neighbor,

Thomas Cameron. Access to discount beef would have been a considerable enticement to Matt Heizer, attempting to compete with four other meat markets.

A brother of Baxter Stingley arrived from Ottawa, Kansas, a few days ago. He is with Cameron & Heizer, the butchers.

The Mountain Mail, November 19, 1881

Enter Jesse Stingley into the suppositions. A skilled butcher, Jesse arrived in Salida that November, having secured employment through his uncle, the Marshal, before coming to town. Baxter Stingley and Edwin Watkins were friends.

Two years later, it was proven that Watkins and his crew stole large numbers of cattle. Suppose Watkins and the elder Cameron were disposing of the stolen beef—the logical thing would be to butcher the cattle and burn the hides quickly. Steaks and other cuts do not carry brands, and besides, who questions the origin of meat at the market? That Jesse would be unaware of the arrangement at some point is illogical for two main reasons. First, working as the butcher, Jesse would probably have had involvement in skinning the cows and could not have failed to notice the changed brands. Second, Jesse swiftly departed Colorado (as discussed in *Chapter Eight*), along with Roe Cameron, Thomas' son, a few months before the murder of Edwin Watkins and the arrest of Ernest Christison—both for cattle rustling.

So back to Matt Heizer. After taking on a business partner, assuming he was unaware of the cattle theft operation, imagine his reaction on learning of the arrangement. Shock? Anger? Righteousness indignation, or perhaps greed—demanding a bigger cut of the profits to remain quiet? These are questions without answers, but the queries are worth pondering.

When Roe Cameron held Matt Heizer at gunpoint on August 13, it could have been pure intimidation—remain quiet or die.

Matt Heizer sold out to Thomas Cameron four months later.

DISSOLUTION NOTICE.

SALIDA, COLO., Dec. 14, 1881.

Notice is hereby given that the co-partnership heretofore existing between Thomas Cameron and Matt Heizer, under the firm name of Cameron & Heizer, is this day dissolved by mutual consent. All accounts due the firm of Cameron & Heizer will be collected by Thomas Cameron, who will pay all debts that the firm owes. T. Cameron & Co. will carry on the meat market at the old stand.

THOMAS CAMERON,
MATT HEIZER.

The Mountain Mail, December 17 1881

T. Cameron & Co.,
MEAT MARKET.

WHOLESALE AND RETAIL

AT

THE LOWEST MARKET PRICE.

On First street, where a good supply of fresh Beef, Pork, Veal, Mutton, Etc., will always be found, both for the WHOLESALE AND RETAIL trade.

They will also keep a full line of

VEGETABLES.

GIVE THEM A CALL.

Salida, - - Colorado.

The Mountain Mail, December 17 1881

Reasonable Questions

Would Jesse Stingley's brother, Baxter, have been unaware of so many cattle's illegal movement and slaughter? Perhaps. It is conceivable that a lawman would not know about such large-scale thievery, even with a family member involved. But based on aggressive actions he later takes to protect Watkins against a group of angry ranchers, it is unlikely. The Stock Growers Association claimed the theft of around $200,000 in cattle (around $5 million today) over a two- to three-year period. They alleged the cattle were taken from the neighboring counties of Fremont and Park to Salida. There is no record or report of any investigation by Salida police or the Chaffee County Sheriff.

Did Matt Heizer sell out to Thomas Cameron because he decided the meat business was not for him? Again, unlikely. Heizer was an experienced butcher and opened a new shop in Salida seven months later with a different partner.

Hollenbeck & Heizer have opened a meat market in the room vacated by Howell. Mat is an old timer and will get his share of the business.

The Mountain Mail, July 10, 1882

CHAPTER FIVE

November 1881
Baxter Stingley Appointed Marshal of Salida

Marshal Baxter Stingley, date unknown

The Mountain Mail, October 30, 1881

October 1881

Appointed Deputy Marshal in October 1881, Baxter Stingley moved up to Marshal several weeks later.

Hollywood often makes the life of a lawman sound glamorous and full of action, but the truth is a Marshal in 1881 spent most of his days chasing stray dogs and telling citizens to clean up the garbage in the street and to pay their dog license fee.

Before Stingley took the job, Salida changed Marshal's every two to three months. Outside of the mundane work of cleaning streets and collecting taxes, most men did not have the guts or the work ethic to run a frontier town. At that time, a peace officer was on call 24/7. There was no personal time or family leave. Day or night, sober or drunk, a Marshal was expected to respond when things happened—even if wearing a nightshirt.

Before Stingley, Marshals regularly left town quietly, usually with a large portion of fines collected for petty crimes. One Officer disappeared on the evening train, claiming to be going after a man he thought had an outstanding warrant. Another got dismissed for embezzlement.

The movies never mention that there was rarely a white hat, upright, morally pure Marshal in the wild west. A good lawman had a bit of outlaw in him, sometimes a lot. Marshals in the 1800s needed toughness, sometimes viciousness, and as the job paid poverty wages, many were involved with side hustles (legal and illegal) to help pay the bills.

Baxter Stingley was no different.

The pay was atrocious—about $2,000 a month in today's money, and the conditions were worse. A frontier Marshal dealt with drunks and violence regularly, often without any backup. To survive, a Marshal had to be considered the toughest man in town.

There is zero doubt that Baxter Stingley was a strong man and a good peacekeeper. Unlike those before him, he never neglected his duties, never ran away from a fight or potential danger, and he did not hesitate to confront outlaws the moment they rode into town. That does not mean Stingley was without sin or that he was averse to looking the other way for friends or family.

~

The day-to-day work of Marshal was often dull and tedious, involving the pursuit of stray dogs or supervising prisoners as they picked up trash from the streets and alleys.

> **Look out for your dogs. Marshal Stingley is on the war path.**

The Mountain Mail, November 12, 1881

> **Mr. Bender has had men on the street this week cleaning up the rubbish in front of his building, Marshal Stingley bossing the job.**

The Mountain Mail, November 26, 1881

~

Society life opened for Baxter Stingley in his new position. A bachelor, he accompanied friends to couples-only events such as the Thanksgiving ball at Maysville. Over 100 couples boarded the special train to attend the party, the largest ever in the region.

~

A few days before Christmas, Marshal Stingley responded to a telegram from the nearby town of Maysville. The Maysville mayor's wife attempted to skip out on a warrant and headed to Salida by train. Stingley met the woman, Mrs. Buck, at the depot to place her under arrest. When he announced his intentions, Mrs. Buck went for her gun, but Stingley drew faster.

Mrs. Buck's arrest warrant was for punching a man in Maysville during an argument at a party. She then drew her gun and forced the man to his knees, and made him apologize for whatever wrong she felt him guilty of.

November 1881—Jesse Arrives

Soon after his appointment to Marshal, Baxter Stingley arranged for his brother, Jesse, to work at the Cameron & Heizer Meat Market, and Jesse relocated to Salida from Ottawa, Kansas.

—Jesse Stingley left Monday for Salida, Chaffee County, Colorado, where he was called by a telegram from his brother, offering him a good situation with a firm there. We wish Jesse succes in his new location.

Independent-Journal, November 24, 1881

A brother of Baxter Stingley arrived from Ottawa, Kansas, a few days ago. He is with Cameron & Heizer, the butchers.

The Mountain Mail, November 19, 1881

Baxter Stingley had a reputation for being a reliable, fair lawman and also as someone not to be messed up. Simply put, he did not abide by rude behavior. His brother, Jesse, working as a meat cutter, appeared to have a similar temperament. In the week before Christmas, placards went up around town, reading "Now for the great mystery." Some men suggested the signs referred to the ingredients in Jesse's sausage (he worked at T. Cameron's Meat Market). The younger Stingley responded with visible anger. A visiting lecturer was so frightened by Jesse's display of fury that he caught the first train out of town. As it turns out, the signs had nothing to do with Jesse Stingley but referred to upcoming entertainment at a local saloon.

One morning this week when our citizens awoke they found the words, "Now for the great mystery," placarded all over town. Some of the boys intimated to Jesse Stingley that the mystery referred to his sausage, and great was his anger thereat. A spiritualist lecturer who happened to be in town was so badly scared that he took the first train for Pueblo. And the next morning when the mystery was solved, and it appeared that it referred to entertainments to be given at Clark & Stewart's saloon the mystery was greater than ever. Who can guess what this last mystery is?

The Mountain Mail, April 15, 1882

The new year of 1882 saw more people entering the thriving town of Salida, and with more arrivals came more crime.

Toward the end of January, about five in the morning, Marshal Stingley was making a final inspection of the jail before turning in for a few hours of needed rest after a busy day and night. To his surprise, he found the doors of the calaboose busted open and the detainees all gone. Escaped was Ruddle, in jail for theft at Marshall Pass, Dooley, in for assaulting his wife, and Reddy, serving time for bruising a female companion.

Stingley suspected that Dooley would be home, which turned out to be true. Dooley claimed the other two men had broken open the door by prying the iron strips off and ordered him out as they left.

Stingley found Reddy in bed with a whore at the Lady Gay Saloon. Ruddle was the only one of the trio serious about escape, having left town without a trace.

> The other evening a couple of Salida's youngsters were talking of "the bad place," and assuming that all would land there eventually one of them said : " Well, if Satan, goes to abusing my mamma, I'll tell Baxter Stingley."

The Mountain Mail, February 4, 1882

On February 18, 1882, Stingley was awakened from sleep by the sound of breaking glass in the building next to his. He rushed outside, quickly captured one man, and soon caught a second suspect in possession of the stolen property. The judge released the two on a $750 bond (around $20,000 today).

~

Modern residents of Salida can give thanks to Marshal Stingley for planting trees throughout town, beginning with those in Alpine Park. Before his arrival, not a single tree existed in the area.

> Marshal Stingley has a force of men at work to-day digging holes to plant trees in and around the city park.

The Mountain Mail, April 15, 1882

Questionable Moment

An early incident that hints at a cloud over the absolute honesty of Marshal Stingley occurred around six in the morning late April 1882.

Stingley was called out of bed by Edward Streepy, who informed the lawman that J.W. Cozad was in a bed at Streepy's dance house and near death. Streepy claimed that a man in his saloon had possession of a watch belonging to Cozad.

Arriving on the scene, Stingley found Cozad in the room, situated above the Clarendon Restaurant. His condition steadily worsened, and he died around nine that night.

The man alleged to have stolen the watch was found and placed under arrest. At the time, he was too drunk to give an account of himself, but after sobering up, the man said the watch had been given to him by Edward Streepy. Stingley immediately issued a warrant for Streepy and a dance house girl, known as 'Curly.'

Friends of Cozad said the man had been drugged and robbed of around three hundred dollars ($5,000 today) in addition to the timepiece. Stingley claimed the watch, stating he loaned it to Cozad. With Cozad dead, no one could challenge the assertion.

The declaration of ownership of the watch is odd for many reasons, not the least of which is that a law enforcement officer in 1882 could rarely afford such luxuries. But no one questioned Stingley's statement, and the pocket watch went to him. Further confusing his contention is that Stingley borrowed a different watch from a friend a few months later.

At a minimum, this incident is odd.

J. W. Cozad Dies Under Suspicious Circumstances.

About six o'clock this morning (Wednesday) Marshal Stingley was called out of bed by Ed. Streepy who informed him that J. W. Cozad was lying at the point of death and that there was a man up at the dance house who had a watch in his possession that had been taken from Cozad.

The marshal got out of bed and went up town to investigate the matter. He found Mr. Cozad at his room over the Clarendon restaurant. Althought assistance had been called in Mr. Cozad continued to grow worse and finally expired about nine o'clock in the forenoon.

The man mentioned by Streepy as having the watch taken from Cozad was found and placed under arrest. At the time he was too drunk to give an account of himself, but afterwards sobered up enough to say that the watch had been given him by Ed. Streepy. Thereupon a warrant was issued for Streepy's arrest and he was taken charge of by deputy sheriff Mix. One of the dance house girls, known as "Curly," was also arrested.

It is claimed by friends of Cozad that he was drugged and robbed of about three hundred dollars in addition to the watch spoken of above. The watch belonged to Stingley and was temporarily in Cozad's possession.

The Mountain Mail, April 29, 1882

Political Aspirations

Baxter Stingley dreamed of greater success, including holding political office. In August 1882, he ran for Salida delegate to the Republican convention but received only eight of the total votes cast.

In November, Stingley got elected constable, receiving nearly 100 votes more than his closest competitor. He beat out James Bathurst, who later served as Stingley's Deputy Marshal.

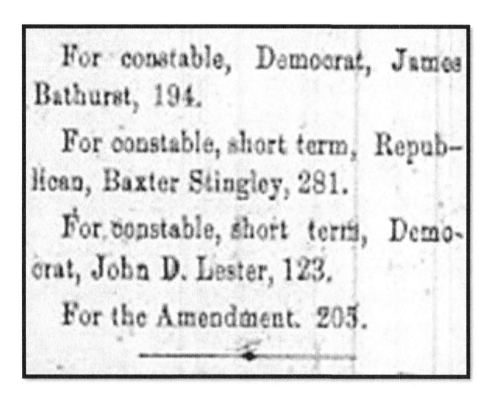

For constable, Democrat, James Bathurst, 194.

For constable, short term, Republican, Baxter Stingley, 281.

For constable, short term, Democrat, John D. Lester, 123.

For the Amendment. 205.

The Mountain Mail, November 11, 1882

CHAPTER SIX

April 1882
Baxter's Brother Marries into a Shady Family

The first solid indication that Baxter Stingley might have a criminal side or be disposed to look away from unlawful activity came on April 7, 1882.

On that day, his brother, Jesse H. Stingley, married Nettie Maria Cameron.

Nettie was the sister of Roe Cameron, the man who, eight months earlier, was part of the cowboy gang that went on a rampage and terrorized the citizens of Salida. He was the same man who held a gun in the face of Matt Heizer, his father's business partner.

Nettie's father, Thomas Cameron, had a role in the Watkins cattle theft operation and later harbored an escaped prisoner (Ernest Christison) in his barn.

Also attending the wedding was Ernest Christison, who Baxter Stingley helped run off his homestead during the Lake County War. Christison was arrested about sixteen months later and convicted of stealing cattle.

> **Married.**
>
> At the residence of Thomas Cameron, Esq., on the evening of April 7, 1882, by B. F. Garrison, J. P., Mr. Jesse H. Stingley to Miss Nettie M. Cameron.
>
> Quite a large number of friends and relatives of the bride and groom were present. Among them were Mr. and Mrs Naylor, Mr and Mrs Cameron, daughter and son of Iowa, Mr. and Miss Coffey, Mr. and Mrs Tom Reed and daughter Rosa, Baxter Stingley, Ernest Christison and all the family of the bride.
>
> The company had a very pleasant time and especially enjoyed the supper, which was a most elegant spread.
>
> The MOUNTAIN MAIL joins with friends of the newly wedded pair in wishing them a long and happy life.

The Mountain Mail, April 15, 1882

Jesse Bush Stingley made the long journey from Kansas to attend his son's wedding. Their mother died years earlier. Baxter had not seen their father since leaving home seventeen years earlier, in 1867.

> Mr. Stingley, father of Baxter and Jesse Stingley of Salida, arrived last night direct from Kansas. Baxter had not seen his father before for seventeen years.

The Mountain Mail, April 29, 1882

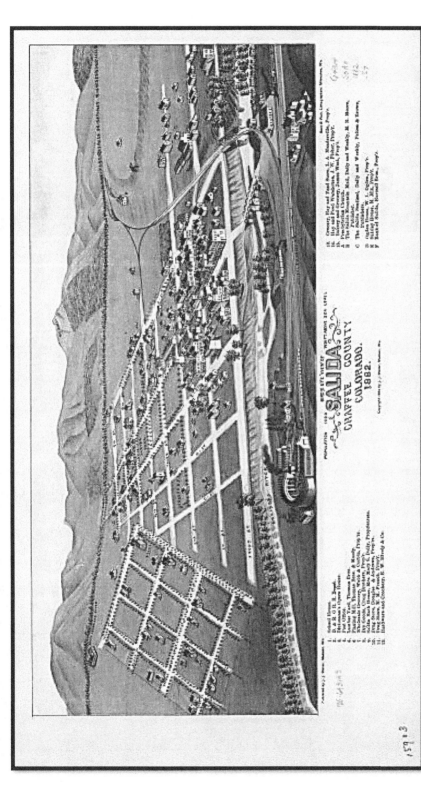

Drawing of Saida, Colorado, 1882
Library of Congress archives

CHAPTER SEVEN

May 30, 1883
A Murder Most Foul

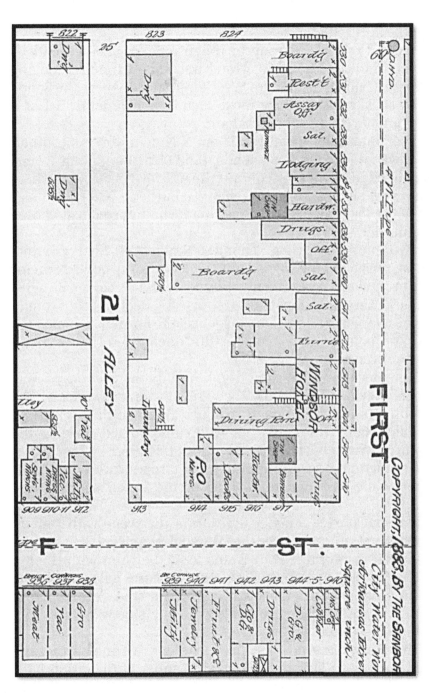

Sanborn Insurance Map, 1883
Library of Congress archives
The Bender Hotel is listed as 'Boarding'

Wednesday, May 30, 1883, was a typical day in Salida. People operated businesses, children attended school, saloons and restaurants were busy, and the ever-present dust covered the entire town.

Around 6 p.m., a group of rough men sat inside Bender's Hotel restaurant. The Bender Hotel was one of the first lodging businesses in Salida, located on West First Street, where the Salida Opera house sits today. Like most such establishments, it had a combination of restaurant and saloon.

The Ninemeyer gang was Thomas Ninemeyer, his brother, Boone, their father, and two friends, Bill O'Brien and Tom Evans. The men lived in the nearby community of Brown's Canyon, where Ninemeyer and Evans worked as charcoal burners. Ninemeyer was known as the local tough guy, a bad man who ran roughshod over the community.

Two months earlier, Thomas Ninemeyer filed criminal charges against a Salida 'shady lady' (which was the polite term for a prostitute), claiming she robbed him. Marshal Baxter Stingley and Deputy Marshal James Bathurst investigated, but the woman denied the charges, and, with no evidence, the lawmen dropped the matter. But that was not satisfactory to Ninemeyer. He was angry and swore revenge.

Ninemeyer and his gang drank heavily the evening of May 30, and as they became drunk, they grew mean and violent. The men shouted they were going to kill the waiter and then screamed they would shoot the cook. Tom Evans walked around the restaurant waving a big knife in the faces of diners.

Hoping to defuse the situation, a railroad worker took over as waiter while Joe Bender, owner of the hotel, sent for the Marshal.

Marshal Baxter Stingley arrived on the scene with Deputy James Bathurst. As soon as the Marshal stepped foot into the Bender Hotel restaurant, Tom Evans lunged at him with the big knife. The Marshal or Deputy Bathurst (witnesses gave conflicting statements) immediately drew a revolver and shot Tom Evans in the chest. Evans staggered outside onto the sidewalk and died.

But this conflict was not over.

The instant the lawmen fired, the entire Ninemeyer gang stood up and began shooting. As one member of the group later admitted, the whole event was a setup designed to start a gunfight with Stingley and his Deputy because the Ninemeyer gang wanted payback for what they saw as an earlier miscarriage of justice.

In the fray, the crew shot Deputy Bathurst in the stomach. He died the following day.

J.D. Gannon, an innocent blacksmith from the railyard, stood from his dinner to run away from the battle, but Thomas Ninemeyer shot him in the chest, and Gannon died instantly.

The outlaw shot Marshal Stingley a few times, on the left side of his chest and the left side of his groin.

Thomas Ninemeyer decided to make a getaway and dashed out the restaurant door, running west on First Street, towards G Street.

Men standing outside heard the shooting. As Ninemeyer sprinted from the scene, two locals tried to stop him, but Ninemeyer shot at them, and they ducked for cover.

A mob of about 50 men quickly got together and chased Thomas Ninemeyer. But he had no intention of being caught and fired several shots in their direction, sending the group scattering for safety.

Ninemeyer turned toward the foothills and kept running.

On the far west side of First Street, a teamster named William Brown watched the scene. When the citizen group ran for cover and stopped chasing Ninemeyer, Brown realized the shooter would escape. So, he borrowed a gun, untied one of his horses, and rode after the criminal. When Brown got within 30 yards of Thomas Ninemeyer, Ninemeyer turned, fired his revolver, and killed William Brown, knocking him from his horse.

Ninemeyer then saw an opportunity immediately—if he could mount the horse, he had a great chance to escape. But the horse was upset by all the gunfire and would not remain still. Before Ninemeyer could calm the animal, three citizens caught up and captured the murderer.

Salida Judge William Hawkins was part of those surrounding Ninemeyer, and the judge shouted they should hang the man right away. The Mayor and the Justice of the Peace were part of the group, and they convinced the angry men to let the law handle the situation, avoiding a lynching.

Nightfall arrived not long after the shootout. Recounting the shootout over drinks, men became enraged over the killings and talked about lynching Thomas Ninemeyer.

The County Sheriff arrived from Buena Vista and worried the drunk men would form a mob and try to hang his prisoner. So, under cover of darkness, the Sheriff sneaked Thomas Ninemeyer to Buena Vista and locked him in the county jail.

But happened to Marshal Baxter Stingley? Well, Stingley was a lucky man that day.

Stingley had borrowed a watch from a friend and had it in his left vest pocket. The bullet struck dead center in the timepiece, saving Baxter Stingley's life. He received a punctured lung from the fragments, but hitting the watch caused the bullet to splinter, and fate spared Baxter Stingley's life.

The Mountain Mail, June 2, 1883

Ninemire's Preliminary Examination.

Thomas Ninemire, the slayer of Bathurst, Brown and Gannon on the evening of May 30, and who has been kept in the Buena Vista Jail since that time for his health, was brought down from the county seat on Monday's train. At the depot he was put in a wagon and accompanied by a heavy guard to Dickman's opera house, where the case was called soon after. Though the trial was public, everybody who desired being admitted to the hall, the officers deemed it best that no one, except the prisoners guard, be admitted who had arms on his person.

The Mountain Mail, June 9, 1883

James H. Bathurst.

The last tribute to a good man when his sands of life have ebbed away is but justice to his worth. No marble monument will hardly rise or storied urns record the traits of character that marked his earthly career. I have known poor "Jim" for many years and knew him well, and to know him as I did was to admire him. His exterior was uncouth, his habits were on the order of fun and mirth, his behavior was unceasing gesture and ready repartee, his conduct in relation to all the higher duties and obligations of life, the climax of honor and good faith. In business his word was an early execution of a promise, a promise not put aside and never unfulfilled. He was a friend under all circumstances, on all sorts of occasions and in all sorts of ways. He never ceased an untiring and constant devotion to those he loved and admired. His word to a friend was the soul of honor exemplified. His affection and devotion to his little son now in Missouri was the mark of a heart within him possessed of the higher order of parental feeling.

His love for the wife that survives him was as illimitable as time. His official conduct was guaged by a feeling of sympathy and mercy. His bravery was proverbial with those who knew him, and to his death he marched with unfaltering tread and met it with no emotion of fear or restraint. These words are not unmeaning flattery, but the sincere sentiments of a devoted friend.   B. F. GARRISON.

The Mountain Mail, June 2, 1883

Remains of the watch that saved Marshal Stingley's life.
On display at the Salida Museum.

CHAPTER EIGHT

August 1883
Cattle Stealing, Lynching, &
the Beginning of the End

A History of Cattle Theft

Almost as soon as cattle arrived in central Colorado, thievery began. The same problem existed anywhere large numbers of cows roamed in vast, unwatched spaces. Sometimes, hungry travelers killed a beef for food, but more often, rustlers moved small numbers (to avoid detection) from their pasture, changed the brand, and quietly built a fortune off the investment and hard work of others. Some operations were more sophisticated, quickly butchering the animals for sale at local meat markets.

This issue of rustling in the region came to a head in August 1883, but signs of trouble appeared two years earlier when breeders, frustrated at losing cattle, began taking matters into their own hands. Among the wealthiest and most formidable ranchers in the area were T. Witcher, Nelson Hallock, William Gibble, Gary Gross, A.J. Bates, and Ira Mulock and his sons, Peter (Pete), Edson (Ed), and Parker (Park).

In October 1881, ranchers caught two men after they shot a couple of cows. Both were arrested and prosecuted.

Cattle Killers Arrested.

For a number of years cattle men in this county have been losing their stock through the scoundrelism of scamps, who were in the habit of shooting cattle promiscuously. Most of the killing was done at the head of Eight Mile creek and from there over as far as Beaver creek. On Tuesday last, while some cow boys were looking after cattle in the hills north of and in sight of town, they saw the flash of a rifle, heard the report and saw an animal fall. They went to the spot and found that one beef belonging to Mulock, one to Witcher and one to Briggs had been shot to death. They soon found the culprits and had J. R. Foster arrested on Wednesday. The other one, Hiram Alden, took his horse and fled, but was overhauled on Thursday by Deputy Sheriff Reub. Frazier at the Hurtsel cabin in Dick's gulch, about fifty miles west of this city.

The Fremont County Record, February 5, 1881

March 1883

Perhaps coincidental, or maybe just staying one step ahead of an impending storm, Jesse Stingley left Salida and returned to Ottawa, Kansas, to open a meat market. There are many possible reasons for the relocation, but convincing his wife to leave her lifelong home and move so far from family and friends is strange. The fact the entire cattle theft operation fell apart five months later adds to the speculation that Jesse Stingley wanted away and fast.

—Jesse Stingley returned from Colorado yesterday, where he has spent the past two or three years. He will "settle down" here now, and go into business, we are glad to learn.

Independent-Journal, March 22, 1883

—Jesse Stingley's wife arrived from Colorado, Tuesday last. They will make Ottawa their future home.

Independent-Journal, April 12, 1883

Jesse H. Stingley & Co., who have purchased John Border's meat market, have taken possession, and will be pleased to receive a continuance of custom at that stand.   tf

Independent-Journal, May 8, 1883

July 9, 1883

Near midnight on July 9, 1883, between the towns of Tin Cup and St. Elmo, an arrest occurred, which triggered a series of events ultimately leading to the murder of Marshal Stingley.

On that night, Deputy Sheriff W.H. Whalen of Tin Cup, and two others, were on a cattle raid. They road late at night to avoid detection from the cattle thieves they hunted. The next morning, the trio found a camp with 75 stolen cows and five men.

Deputy Whalen was experienced and savvy and followed the letter of the law by not accusing anyone without solid proof. Alone, he rode into the camp without a gun. Whalen carried decoy brands instead of a weapon and claimed to be searching for stray horses. Confirming his suspicions, Whalen rode back to St. Elmo and told local ranchers he had located stolen cattle. But Whalen needed someone to swear out a warrant before he could make a legal arrest.

Preparing to return to the cattle camp, the Mulock brothers rode into town and said they would accompany the Deputy as the brands he saw belonged to them. The Deputy was reluctant to move forward without an official warrant. The Mulock brothers told him the Cattle Association of Colorado was all the backing he needed, and off they rode.

The Deputy arrested two of the five separately when he found them riding alone. Then, he went into the camp and asked the remaining three men who owned the cattle. The leader, Ernest Christison, said he was the titleholder. The three reached for guns, but Deputy Whalen drew his first, covered them all, and waited for the Mulock brothers and the other ranchers to arrive. Two cattlemen drove the herd to Fairplay as the stolen stock was from nearby Middle Park in Park County. The arrested men were taken into town and jailed.

On closer examination, thieves changed the cattle brands, but they did a sloppy job, and the original imprints were easy to read.

EXCITING CAPTURE

Of Cattle Thieves as Narrated by Deputy
Sheriff Whalen of Tin Cup.

Following are the full particulars of the
pursuit and capture of the cattle thieves, by
W. H. Whalen, per announcement in yesterday's REVIEW-PRESS:

Abbeyville, July 9, 1883.

*John H. Bowman, Esq., Sheriff of Gunnison
county, Colorado:*

DEAR SIR:—I returned yesterday from my
cattle thief raid. I went over the range on
Wednesday night at 12 o'clock, so that no
one would get on my "racket." I took Dave
Corsaut and John Scott with me. The next
morning I took a man with me from St. Elmo
that had some mules up in the range, and I
rode about twenty-five miles that forenoon
and found seventy head of cattle, the cattle
thieves camp and five men. I then rode into
their camp alone and left my gun behind, as
I did not want to arouse any suspicion, and
wanted to get the lay of the ground and the
description of the men. I had some decoy
brands to show them, as I represented that I
was looking for stray horses. I then returned to St. Elmo and reported to three of the
cattle association men that was there with
me what I had discovered, and they
said the cattle were stolen and that
they wanted the men, and I was
just going to start to capture them when
the Mulock Brothers rode up. I then reported
to them what cattle and brands and men I
had found, and they said it was their cattle
and they wanted the men. I then started

and took the cattle men around the theives camp and brought them into the cattle two miles above the thieves camp, and the first bunch of cattle we came to had twenty-four head in and fifteen of them was the Mulock Brothers brand. They then said they wanted the thieves. I then asked them what my backing was as I had no warrant, and they told me the cattle association of Colorado was my backing. I then took Uncle Dave and started for the camp, and told the cattle men to keep in supporting distance, about one-fourth of a mile in my rear. I had not gone over a quarter of a mile before I saw one of the band making for the timber. I charged up and took him in; about one-half a mile further on I took another; then I rode into their camp of three men and asked them who owned the bunch of cattle. The leader said he owned them and his name was Earnest Christian. They then saw our guns and they started for their guns, but too late, for I covered them and held them till the cattle man came up. The cattle (?) took them to Fairplay, as the cattle were stolen from Middle Park. They wanted me to go through with them, but on account of court matters at home did not go, but turned them over to Uncle Dave, and they went on through to Fairplay. They told me to put two men in charge of the cattle, which I did, and then came home and as yet have not heard the result from them.

Several parties have skipped out since the arrest of the thieves and the associotion are after them. There was a large organized band of them.   W. H. WHALIN,
Deputy Sheriff at Tin Cup.

Later in July 1883

Many ranchers suspected their stolen cattle were at Edwin Watkins's place because of Watkins associates, employees, and business partners, including the recently arrested Christison. It is safe to assume that rumors or suspicions involved Watkins's neighbor, Thomas Cameron, and his meat market in Salida.

Following the arrest of Ernest Christison, three ranchers rode to Watkins's ranch to check for other purloined cattle. Watkins met the cattlemen with a rifle. The men demanded that he ride his 80-acre spread and show them the brands, but Watkins refused, saying he had other obligations. He invited the rancher to look over the property as they pleased. The suspicious men examined the stock and counted 120 head of cattle, 30 of which they said wore brands not owned by Watkins. At gunpoint, they removed the cows from Watkins's ranch.

"In June of the present summer Watkins, Christison and Fuller dissolved partnership and divided the stock on hand. Fuller allowed his part to remain with Watkins, while Christison drove his portion, about seventy head, over on Chalk Creek, above St. Elmo, and there stopped until the snow should disappear and allow their passage over the range to the western slope. At that point Christison and party were arrested and taken to Fairplay, where Christison gave bonds in $1,500, but has not yet been tried and will not be until the September term. The cattle in his possession belonged to Nelson Hallock, Mr. Gribble, Mulock Brothers and others, and were recovered by the owners. About a month ago three cattle men went to Watkins' ranch to examine his cattle and were met by him with a Winchester rifle in hand. They asked him to go and show them the cattle in his field, but he said he was just about going away and could not go with them. However, he told them where the cattle could be found, and they rode in that direction. The cattle found in Mr. Watkins' field numbered about 120, bearing a variety of brands, ninety of which were claimed by him."

The Fairplay Flume, August 23, 1883

The Mulock Clan

Before proceeding with this story, it is necessary to provide an overview of the most influential cattleman involved, including his reach.

Ira Mulock of Fremont County was one of the wealthiest men in the region, President of a bank, a county representative at the State convention, and owner of more cattle than any other rancher. He did not hesitate to use lawsuits against opponents, nor did he shrink from resorting to violence. (See *Chapter Thirteen* for details). His three sons, Peter, Edson, and Parker, ran his ranch and enforced their father's desires.

IRA MULOCK, President.   JOSHUA MULOCK, Vice President.

A. R. GUMAER, Cashier.

MULOCK BROS. & CO.,

EXCHANGE BANK

Of Canon City, Colorado.

Transact a General Banking Business.

Will buy and sell Eastern and Foreign Exchange, and Discount Approved Paper at Reasonable Rates.

Collections will Receive Prompt Attention.

The Fremont County Record, August 13, 1882

The primary convention, for the purpose of electing delegates from precinct No, 1 to the county convention, was held in Sanders' hall Wednesday afternoon. O. G. Stanley presided and W. H. McClure was secretary. Short speeches were made by Mess. Stanley and E. B. Alling. Col. Sawyer, Capt. Ferrier and S. R. Baldwin were appointed to name the delegates and the following gentlemen were selected: Jas. Clelland, E. B. Alling, W. A. Stump, M. Dueber, R. Jeske, W. H. McClure, O. G. Stanley, J. J. Phelps, G. O. Baldwin and Ira Mulock.

The Fremont County Record, September 13, 1882

WHEREAS—There is among the laws of Cañon an ordinance authorizing the taking up, fining and selling of stock running at large in the city limits, and

WHEREAS—The geography of the country is such that stock passing from the mountains to the plain, back and forth, are compelled to pass through Cañon, there being no herd-law in this portion of Colorado, and

WHEREAS—The above ordinance has been enforced in such a way as to cause seizure, fining and sale of stock running and belonging in the country around Cañon, thus working injustice and loss to a class of men representing one of the principal industries of the state, therefore be it

Resolved—By the stock-men whose names appear below, that we do hereby petition the Honorable Town Board of Cañon to so amend said law as to in no way interfere with stock which do not habitually run in town, and which therefore cannot rightly be regarded a nuisance.

That while we desire to do nothing contrary to law we are determined to at once respect the rights of all our fellow citizens and protect our own.

R M Pope	Ira Mulock
P A Rice	Obe Spurlock
Henry Thompson	Jim Sims
Henry Beckham	John Bender
R A Gardner	Sam Wear
Mart Gardner	John McGuire
Len Gardner	Ed Benedict
Jo Hall	Al Haggart
Geo Fear	Lon Reid
S M Cox	Jim Priest
John Binkley	X B Reid
Jim McGee	O P Allen
Fred Cornell	E L Taylor
John Sweet	Clint Sampson
Levi Longfellow	Silas Pollock
H L White	R Munn
Will Hammond	Will Webster
Harry Catlin	H L Belknap
Los Sampson	J R Witcher
John D Clark	Jesse Kelly
T Witcher	M D DeHoney
H M Buroughs	W C Catlin
Geo H Green	Wm Curtis
T J Toug	H W Hodges
M Mills Craig	J A Adams
Charles Pauls	C E Mulock
Eady Bros	Jas Locke

The Fremont County Record, December 10, 1881

August 1883—Standoff in Salida

Edwin Watkins claimed he owned the stock legally and swore out a warrant for theft against the ranchers—T. Witcher, William Gribble, L. Sampson, the Mulock brothers, and Gary Gross.

As the accused cattlemen exited the train in Salida to face arraignment in court, they were surprised when Deputy Sheriff Miles Mix immediately confronted them.

Mix was a well-connected, original settler of Salida. A former County Commissioner and Justice of the Peace, he was both friend and political running mate of Baxter Stingley. Mix also operated a saloon, Mix House, and a brickyard in 1882. Frank Reed worked at the brickyard when he was not a cowpuncher.

Miles Mix had many of Edwin Watkins friends with him and threatened to kill the ranchers the first chance he had, but the cattlemen played it cool and did not say a word or do anything to start a fight.

Marshal Baxter Stingley soon arrived on the scene, backing Mix and the friends of Watkins. He told the ranchers to keep their mouths shut and leave town as soon as the hearing was over. The cattlemen did as Stingley ordered. When their hearing concluded, they hopped on the evening train and returned to South Park.

The Mountain Mail, January 15, 1881

Let Republicans not lose sight o[f] the precinct ticket in their efforts to give the State and county ticket a large majority. The whole Republican ticket will be ahead in this precinct, but the fect that Pomeroy, Stingley and Mix are so much the superiors of their opponents ought to inspire the Republicans with a great deal of zeal in their behalf.

The Mountain Mail, November 4, 1882

Miles Mix has succeeded A. T. Ryan as deputy sheriff in this precinct.

The Mountain Mail, January 21, 1882

replevin suit. They were met at the depot by one Mix, of Salida, and keeper of one of the worst gin mills and gambling saloons of the town, and the principal headquarters for thieves, and a crowd of his followers, sympathizers with Watkins and his gang, who abused them in the most shameful manner, and threatened to kill them at the first opportunity, without the slightest provocation being offered by the cattle men, who kept quiet and wisely refused to join in a row with this mob. After transacting their business they followed the advice and request of Baxter Stingley, the town marshal, and departed on the evening train for South Park. The following Wednesday, Aug. 15, the same men having to appear at Salida to answer in the criminal action instituted by Watkins, and taking the request of the marshal of two days before as a confession on the part of the town authorities of their inability to protect them against the threatened action of the mob, came with a body of about thirty-five armed men, made up of cattle owners like themselves, who had come from the extreme limits of South Park, with their cow boys, determined to protect the defendants and themselves from attack. Not wishing, however, to create

The Fairplay Flume, August 30 1883

Old Friends

Perhaps unknown to the ranchers, Edwin Watkins and Baxter Stingley were friends. The two men often shared time in a local saloon, and they once lived together.

August 15, 1883

The ranchers returned to Salida the following Monday, August 15, for their trial, but they prepared to battle this time, bringing thirty-five gunmen as protection. Whether or not the cattlemen knew of the friendship between Baxter Stingley and Watkins, they had figured out that the law was not going to protect them in Salida.

After exiting the train, the livestock farmers sent word to the Marshal that their guns were for safety, not a fight. They wanted to be sure there was no misunderstanding.

Stingley sent word back telling the men to stay at the Monte Christo Hotel until the following day. And that was what the ranchers did. They avoided the saloons, remained quiet, and laid low, being polite and respectful to everyone.

The next day, after breakfast, the ranchers waited at the hotel until 2 p.m. when the trial was to begin. Then they made the long walk down F Street, about three blocks to the location of the hearing, Craig's Opera House. Stingley had the group disarm but provided 15 guards to ensure their safety. A large group of local ranchers joined the procession to provide extra security.

The criminal cases are set for Augus' 15, at which time Mr. Watkins wil show that the cattle were his, and that they were taken from him by force upon the sheer statement of parties who have been trying to crush Mr. Cameron and Mr. Watkins from the range for years. Mr. Watkins has borne a reputa

The Mountain Mail, August 11, 1883

Tables Turned

Edwin Watkins lost his lawsuit when the court ruled the cattle on his ranch did not belong to him and refused to indict the accused cattlemen.

Before the trial, T. Witcher had sworn a warrant in Fremont County, where Witcher held his power base. Immediately after the dismissal of all charges against him, Witcher informed the court of his order, which demanded the arrest of Edwin Watkins, Frank Reed, and Ernest Christison for stealing cattle. The judge had Watkins arrested on the spot and transported to Canon City for arraignment. Reed and Christison were not present.

The grand jury of Chaffee county refused to indict Waugh, Witcher, Gribble and the Mulock boys, but indicted Chris ison and Reed, cattle thieves who were companions of Watkins.

The Sierra Journal, September 27, 1883

L. E. Watkins Hanged by a Gang of Blood-thirsty Cow Boys.

The Denver *Republican's* correspondent gives the following account of the horrible killing of L. E. Watkins at Canon City on the morning of the 11th:

"T. Witcher, of this county, swore out a complaint before Justice Minner, July 27, for the arrest of L. E. Watkins, a cattle man residing in the upper part of the county near the Chaffee county line, charging Watkins with stealing several cattle belonging to Mullock Brothers and others and mutilating the brands.

The Delta Chief, August 22, 1883

Watkins Lynched

During the trial for stealing 18 cows, the same cows he filed a lawsuit for in Salida and lost, Edwin Watkins told the judge he had papers proving he paid for the cattle and asked to be allowed to return home and retrieve the evidence.

The judge thought the request was fair and ordered the Sheriff to go with Watkins by train to his ranch outside of Salida, so the defendant could get the papers he claimed would prove his innocence.

After the trip to his ranch, Edwin Watkins and the Sheriff returned to Canon City on the midnight train. As the two men walked in the dark from the depot to Canon City, over a dozen masked men rushed out of the shadows. A few of the gang grabbed the Sheriff and said he would not be hurt if he kept quiet.

Edwin Watkins received no such a guarantee.

When they cut Edwin Watkins's body down the next morning—it was hanging from the bridge—a savage act had unmistakably occurred.

The coroner stated that Watkins was shot in the right breast, the gunshot coming from above, meaning Watkins was lying on the ground when murdered. The evidence indicated Edwin Watkins was dead before he was hanged and thrown over the side of the bridge.

No record shows whether Watkins carried proof of his innocence.

Frank Reed was a partner in Edwin Watkins's cattle operation. After Watkins's murder, Reed stated in public that he wanted to meet the Marshal tough enough to arrest him because he would never be taken alive.

Despite a $250 reward from the Governor, no one ever identified the murderers of Edwin Watkins—the investigation was quietly and quickly dropped.

Six months later, in February 1884, T. Witcher was elected Treasurer of the Stockman Association. In March, he was appointed a round-up commissioner by Colorado Governor Grant.

All the court records of the case against Edwin Watkins disappeared shortly after his murder.

THERE seems a probability that the mob who lynched L. E. Watkins, at Canon City, will be apprehended and brought to justice. The Mulock brothers, of whom there are three, Pete, Ed. and Park, are suspected of having had something to do with the crime. An investigation is in progress, and it is hoped the guilty parties will be apprehended and punished.

Carbonate Chronicle, August 18, 1883

Stingley Swears Revenge

At the time of the lynching of Edwin Watkins, Marshal Baxter Stingley was in Texas on business. He hopped on the first train back to Salida, where he swore vengeance on whoever murdered his friend.

imagined. Watkins was a quiet fellow. He very rarly frequented saloons, and never drank anything but cider and ginger ale or some ligbt drink of a non-intoxicating nature. He did not even use tobacco, and I was never more surprised in my life than when I heard he was accused of cattle stealing Stingley was just the opposite. So for as I know, he was a good man, but he drank and went with the boys, and possessing just the qualities which were objective to Watkins, and living in the same house with him, they became fast friends. In fact, they were so firm in their friendship that when Watkins was lynched, Stingley, who was in Texas, registered an oath to avenge his death, and started back to Salida to fulfill it.''

Carbonate Chronicle, December 15, 1883

Lauren Edwin Watkins, 1853-1883

Cattlemen Defend Murder

Less than two weeks after the murder of Edwin Watkins, cattlemen in the region hired former Governor Pitkin as legal counsel. They organized a formal group, United Rocky Mountain Cattle Growers Association, and published an open letter defending the killing. There was no denial that Watkins got murdered or that ranchers had committed the killing. The letter stated the membership was "...unanimous in giving express to a sense of relief at his 'removal' from the ranges..."

> . On Monday there was a gatl e:ing of stock growers at Poncha Springs that representd one and a quarter millions of dollars investment in that business. The partial account of the proceedings sent the FLUME is so incomplete that we have had recourse to the dailies for some of the details.
>
> Harry Van Kleeck, a large cattle owner in Chaffee county, was selected to preside and John A. Eddy, of this county was elected secretary. During the morning session steps were taken to organize the Rocky Mountain Stock Grower's association, the object as stated by ex-Governor Pitkin and others, being mutual protec- tion from cattle thieves. Delegates from

tion from cattle thieves. Delegates from each of the neighboring counties were chosen as follows: For Park county, J. A. Eddy, Mac. Bates and Wm. Hammond. Fremont county, C. Sampson, Henry Belknap and R. C. McCoy. Chaffee county, Wm. Champ, Wm. White, H. Van Kleeck, John Mundlein, Otis White, T. H. Brown and Messrs. Ashpaugh and Bales. Saguache county, A. Shellaberger, C. R. Hartman, G. H. Adams, T. A. Young and W. T. Ashby. A committee on organization consisting of Messrs. Bates, Sampson, Champ and Shellabarger was appointed, and another committee on resolutions was made up of Messrs. Eddy, Belknap, Bales and Adams. Pending the report of this latter committee the convention adjourned until afternoon and informally prepared the following document for general publication:

"There has existed in Chaffee county for several years an organized gang of cattle thieves, who have stolen cattle from cattle owners and ranchmen on the Arkansas and South Arkansas valleys and off the Cameron hills along the southwest limits of the South Park, until over $200,000 worth of cattle have been taken or driven out of Chaffee county alone, not to mention the value of the stock taken from Park, Fremont and Saguache county ranges. These depradations were at first committed secretly, a few head of stock being driven off or killed in some remote mountain fastness and the meat marketed through some friendly butcher shop in the nearest valley towns and mining camps, but of late, immunity from punishment has so emboldened the thieves, that they have driven from these ranges entire bunches of cattle and horses; in one case eighty head of cattle, in another seventy head, in another fifty-eight head of horses; disfigured and altered their brands, and then have coolly driven them at leisure across the country, inviting inspection and challenging discovery.

As to the lynching of Watkins, the cattle and ranch men and the best citizens of this section of the country are unanimous in giving expression to a sense of relief at his "removal" from the ranges in this vicinity. While deprecating the condition of affairs which renders it necessary for the cattle men to take such violent measures for the protection of their property, large sums of money have been expended in Chaffee county in the prosecution of the thieves with no beneficial results. Not only is it difficult to secure legal proof against such a well organized and experienced gang of thieves, but even after securing a conviction, as in the case of Redcliff and McPherson, the men are still at large and it has become evident that the law is too slow and too uncertain to meet the emergencies of the situation. The thieves themselves laugh at the idea of prosecution, and they have been riding the ranges in squads prepared to "down" any cattle man who might attempt simply to recover his cattle. In their boldness and sense of security from punishment they have gone so far as to threaten the lives of several of the men who have been the most prominent in the recent arrests and prosecutions. Is it to be wondered at that under such circumstances law-abiding, peace-loving men resort to desperate measures to secure protection for their lives and their property? It is to be regretted that the public has been is to be regretted that the public has been misinformed through the activity and the shrewdness of Watkins' friends, the parties most interested in first gaining the ear of the press, as to the real condition of affairs culminating in his death at Canon City, and as to his character and that of his associates.

JOHN MUNDLEIN, H. C. HONNELL,
T. H. BROWN, W. D. WHITE,
J. T. ASHBOUGH, W. H. CHAMP,
WM. BALE, ORIS WHITE,
H. VAN KLEECK, WM. MATTHEWS,

During the afternoon session resolu-

The Fairplay Flume, August 30, 1883

September 1883

The Cattle Growers Association held its first convention in Poncha Springs. Many ranchers spoke openly about Edwin Watkins and his gang, claiming that cattle thieves had operated freely in Chaffee County for some time, stealing over $200,000 of livestock (about $5 million today). The cattlemen said the thieves were clever, stealing only 60 or 70 head at a time, but they found it odd that no one had ever been caught or punished.

The main reason for the group meeting was to prepare documentary evidence for charges they expected against the most influential members.

T.H. Robbins, President of the South Park Cattle Grower's Association, published a letter in the *Denver Republican* (sadly, there are no surviving archives) stating the lynching of Edwin Watkins was a just punishment.

T. H. Robbins, president of the South Park Cattle Grower's Association, publishes an open letter in the Denver *Republican* in which he boldly asserts that the hanging of L. E. Watkins was a just punishment for his repeated thefts of stock. He gives dates and places where stock belonging to other owners were driven off and butchered by Watkins and his men, and others where considerable numbers were found in their possession. The details are very full and the charges explicit.

The Delta Chief, September 5, 1883

Public Outrage

Outside of those associated with ranching, the media and most citizens were furious over Watkins's murder. They were also incensed that cattlemen did not deny the killing and that no one was ever prosecuted for the crime.

> The meeting of the Cattle Growers association calls to mind the fact that the murderers of young Watkins have not yet been brought to justice and that, to the lasting disgrace of Fremont county, they probably never will be.

Leadville Daily Herald, January 6, 1884

IT is a sad commentary on justice when men, who happen to have a little money, can brutally murder a man who has simply been suspected of stealing, and then defy the courts to bring them to justice. This is the shape matters are in at Salida. It is not known that Watkins was guilty of stealing cattle. He was under arrest for having replevined cattle which he claimed as his own, and which the brands showed to be his own, and while under arrest, he was taken from the officer and murdered by a mob. The mob now attempts to justify its act by saying $200,000 worth of cattle had been stolen from them by a gang of twenty experienced thieves, of which Watkins was the leader. If this were true, there is no justification for their act of murder. And it is just probable that it is not true. Watkins was prosperous in his business and at his death left his widow but $3,000. If the Cattle Growers' Association are correct in their statement, he should have been worth not less than $10,000 from his stealings alone, aside from his legitimate business—which would aggregate $13,000 —and as ''the leader of the gang'' he should have had still more. We trust the press of this state will not let this crime, this terrible and unjustifiable crime, go unpunished. If it cannot itself execute the law, it can at least keep the matter alive until the authorities shall do something, despite the well filled purses of this association. Never was there a blacker crime in the state, and its perpetrators, too, claiming to be respectable men. Al. Packer's crime was an honor compared with it. Packer killed his companions to eat them. His provocation was excessive hunger. It was kill them or die himself. But the crime of which these men are guilty had no provocation. They were not willing the courts should take their course, because they claim they could not get justice in the courts. It would be a more fitting way for them to say it had they said they

could not get the kind of law in the courts they wanted—lynch law. Had they convicted their enemy the punishment would have been penitentiary, and that they did not want. They wanted blood, and they got it. Watkins' blood is upon their hands, and the state will rest under disgrace so long as they go unpunished. Because they are men of means should be no excuse for their escape. So much greater is the shame. It adds corruption, bribery, to the monumental villainy. They say Watkins' murder was right, it was justice. Let them come into court and say ''we are guilty.''

Carbonite Chronicle, September 8, 1883

Thomas Cameron

Following the murder of Edwin Watkins, Thomas Cameron closed his meat market in Salida. He remained in town working his farm.

Notice for Publication.

Land Office at Leadville, Colorado, }
August, 21st 1884. {

NOTICE IS HEREBY GIVEN that the following-named settler has filed notice of her intention to make final proof in support of her claim, and that said proof will be made before the Judge of Chaffee county at Buena Vista, Colorado, on September 22d, 1884, viz: Mary F. Watkins, D. S. No. 2782, for the s ½ nw ¼ section 25, township 50 north range 8 east N. M. Mer. She names the following witnesses to prove her continuous residence upon, and cultivation of, said land, viz: J. T. Watkins, M. H. Watkins, Thomas Cameron, Wm. Cantonwine, all of Salida, Chaffee county, Colorado. S. J. HANNA.
Register.
First pub. Aug. 23, 1884—Last pub. Sep. 20, 1884.

Public Noticed of Proof of Improvement for Homestead Patent, noting Watkins and Cameron as neighbors.
The Mountain Mail, November 3, 1883

Jesse Stingley

To solidify the case that Jesse Stingley was probably part of the cattle theft and butchering organization, Jesse left Salida months before Watkins's killing, returning home to Kansas. He may not have felt safe even back home because he was preparing to move to the Washington Territory when his brother, Baxter, was murdered. Jesse Stingley did not return to Colorado until 1885 and stayed out of Salida until 1893.

Roe Cameron joined Jesse Stingley in the flight from Salida and also sought refuge in the northwest. He was not back in Colorado until the 1900 United States Census.

The very atmosphere to day appears burdened with gloom and sadness on account of the death of Marshal Stingley. He was born in the state of Iowa about 38 years ago, and leaves a father who is now living at Ottawa, Kansas, and a brother, Jessie Stingley, who was about starting to Washington Territory from Ottawa, to look up a new home, and a married sister who is living in Missouri, and also an uncle, Moses Stingley, who was living at Sweet Home, in above state. Baxter

Carbonate Chronicle, September 8, 1883

Mary Watkins

After the murder of her husband, Mary Watkins filed a lawsuit against T. Witcher, a Cotopaxi, Colorado rancher. Witcher was one of the men who took cows from Edwin Watkins ranch—the ones for which he faced charges. Witcher was also the man who filed charges against Watkins for stealing cattle.

Mrs. Watkins won her lawsuit, which stated that her husband was the rightful owner of nine cows. She was awarded $225 (about $5,000 today) and planned other legal action, but, probably due to threats she alluded to in a letter, she soon sold the family ranch and left the Arkansas Valley.

Before leaving the region, Mrs. Watkins wrote a lengthy scathing letter to the editor, naming names and claiming powerful ranchers, including Ira Mulock and his sons, conspired with Sheriff Johnson of Fremont County to murder her husband to cover the tracks of their crimes.

Mrs. Watkins, whose husband was lynched at Canon City for alleged cattle stealing, brought suit against T. Witcher to recover the value of nine head of cattle taken by Witcher and others before the lynching and upon which it is alleged, the charge which resulted in Watkins' death was based. She was awarded $225, and other suits are expected to follow.

The Sun, March 15, 1884

Burning Words from the Prophetic Pen of the Wife of the Murdered Watkins,

IN REPLY TO THE CATTLE MEN.

"Men Who Have Murdered the Law Cannot Appeal to the Law."

Mrs. Mary F. Watkins, the widow of the murdered man, and an ex-school-mistress of Ohio, has written a reply to the statement made by the United Rocky Mountain Cattle Raisers' association, in which they endeavored to justify the murder of Watkins. It is as follows:

To the Murderers of My Husband:

Your recent report to the Cattle Men's association at Poncha Springs is such a flagrant misstatement of well-known facts, such a feeble avoidance of all the important issues in the case, such a clumsy effort to draw the public gaze away from the blood upon your hands, such a contemptible trick to shift the expenses of the trials you will soon (I hope) be put upon from your own pockets to the treasury of the Cattle Men's association, such an imbecile purpose to frighten justice and stay the descending hand of the law by the blatant announcement that you represent nearly two million dollars' worth of cattle and that you will act together in this defense. All this is in my opinion such an ill-advised step that, murderers though you are, I wonder you should be fools enough to take it. First, you say: ''L. E. Watkins was lynched by a mob.'' The people of Canon have given you the lie on that point. They say it was not a mob, but a cowardly gang of men after private vengeance. A mob means some effort at justice. You did not murder my husband to get justice, but to prevent it. A mob means some expression of public sentiment. Public sentiment, even in your own town, repudiates your crime and brands you with the brand of Cain. You say you had ''overwhelming evidence'' of my husband's guilt. Are you fools enough to expect the public to take the word of murderers on that point? If you had ''overwhelming evidence,'' why did you not let it appear in your own court in Fremont county, where the murdered man had neither friends nor influence, where court officers friendly to your leaders would have summoned a jury certain to convict on even evidence far less than overwhelming?

You say the cattle with the alleged altered brands were ''discovered'' in Watkins' possession. You know better, all his neighbors know better. You know that when accused of having your cattle, he rounded up his little heard of his own accord and invited you to come and cut out the stolen cattle if you could find any. You know that when you could not agree among yourselves with any certainty, and that an experienced Kansas cattle man, an expert judge of brands, declared he did not believe the brands had been altered. In spite of this, and to make out a case for yourselves, you drove off twenty-one head. Five of these he admitted were not his, but as to sixteen he protested and forbade you to drive them off. You say he had the ''audacity to sue a writ of repleven'' at once and to have you arrested.

But, pray, is not a writ of replevin the legal means of recovering property wrongfully taken? Did he not keep within the law, while you went outside of it? You have tried to show that he was a high-handed outlaw. Yet his neighbors and friends would have shot you down like dogs that day for your outrage only that relying on the law he would not allow it. He invited you to dinner and some of you came and ate with him, and soon after murdered him.

You have made the preposterous statement that he stole with his gang over $200,000 worth of cattle. Who will believe this or any part of it that knew what an industrious, saving man your victim was, and yet how poor, leaving but two or three thousand dollars' worth of property? How do you account for the wide difference between the facts and your statement.

You say that he was hung by a mob of "unknown" masked men. You know he was not hung at all. He was murdered and his dead body tied by the neck to the bridge—that was all. "Unknown men," you say. Uunknown to whom, pray? Not generally unknown in Canon and Cotopaxi; not entirely unknown to me. One of them (I hear) is positively known to Sheriff Jones. All of them, I think, are well known to Deputy Sheriff Johnson; to Ira Mulock and his sons; to Justice Banta, of Cotopaxi, who is reported to have said, "John and me helped hang the s— of a b—;" to Brown; to Champ; and to Van Kleeck, of the Poncha Springs committee, and to others whose names I cannot now call up. Yes, there is one more who knows you all. I allude to General Cook, of the Rocky Mountain Detective agency. This may be important for you to remember.

You boast that if arrested you cannot be convicted. I grant that, as to the present, and I understand from General Cook that that is the reason you have not been arrested. You control the working machinery of the court—or at least you think you do, but possibly you are mistaken. You found yourselves woefully mistaken about your control of the newspapers of Canon, which all spoke up manfully and branded you in spite of your threats. You may be convinced yet. Justice is slow; meanwhile conscience, as I think you know, is swift. Though all of you have shown yourselves a cowardly, merciless, God-defying gang, some of you, I think, are not so brutish but you have a conscience. The shadow of the man you have murdered will keep you company, and will be with you in lonely places. You will suddenly discover his blood upon your doorposts some day, and the shame with which you vainly tried to cover him will overwhelm your children. May I remind you that one murderer was recently sentenced to death in Colorado after having escaped the law nine years? There is a reward upon your heads. It will be to the interest of some who know you now to keep track of you.

You have tried to make out that my husband was a low, illiterate man, of bad origin and of an evil life. I know that he was a very fairly educated man, who, though of poor parents, was yet related to one of the governors of Ohio. As to his evil life you only make that statement for places where he was not known.

I am still on the ranch. You may murder me (I do not think you are above it), but as long as I live I shall defend the name of my dead, and though you are probably too strong for me, with the funds of the association behind you, the day will come when I shall catch you. You have robbed me of a kind and loving husband. You have robbed a poor, aged father of his only son. Behold your work and examine your hands! Waiting patiently for justice, and invoking the shadow of your crime upon you, I am,

MRS. MARY F. WATKINS.

ANOTHER STATEMENT.

In addition to the above, Mrs. Watkins addressed a letter to the Denver Tribune, from which we take the following:

* * * I wish also to return my tearful thanks to the innumerable host of friends (especially to the disinterested friends at Canon) who in resenting this cowardly outrage on the laws and the justice of Fremont county, have also comforted and supported me under this cruel, cruel blow by their most kind sympathy. It is only natural that I should wish all these people to feel as sure of my husband's innocence as I do myself. His kind, manly heart they cannot know, but they can see how quietly and fearlessly he gave himself into the hands of the law, and how these men, his personal enemies because he had crossed them in business matters, seeing that the law would not answer their cruel ends, (justice not being what they wanted, but blood) although they had him in their own county, where he, if guilty, could expect no leniency from court or jury, yet they murdered him before he could get a trial, although they say in their Poncha Springs resolution that they had ''the most overwhelming evidence of his guilt.''

Dear friends at Canon and Salida, kind people whose sympathy has supported me through all this bitter trial, you could not know my poor, courageous, manly boy as I knew him; you could not be sure of his innocence as I, his old school fellow, his sweetheart, his wife, and—oh! it breaks my heart to say it—his widow, am sure of it, but you know when men state such an improbable fact as that they have "overwhelming proof," and yet refuse to let that proof be heard in their own court, they must be lying. You have been kind to me, you have been tender with my dead, and I will not doubt you will take my solemn assurance for it when I say I know he was innocent, and that the real cause of his cruel murder was a bitter personal enmity growing largely out of his having gotten the start of some of these parties in a fair business rivalry. They are domineering, wilful men, who could not bear this, and thus persecution has grown apace and has ended in their imbruing their hands in his blood. They saw that he was cool and courageous and kept to the right, and could not be coaxed nor intimidated. They saw that all his neighbors and men everywhere liked him and found him square in his deal, keeping his word and paying his debts everywhere. They saw that the arrows of suspicion, so maliciously fired at him, would not stick, and that they could not fasten an infamous crime upon him, even in their own court, and by their own "overwhelming testimony." They make the preposterous charge, in their report to the Cattle Men's association at Poncha Springs, that within five years he has been the means of having $200,000 worth of cattle stolen from them. They charge him with being the leader of a gang of about twenty, and a very dangerous character! The simplest facts disprove this falsehood. As the leader of such a gang, stealing such a sum, his share could not be less than $10,000, while as a *leader* it ought to be much more.

My husband was a man of simple and inexpensive habits, quiet, never drinking, never running with fast young men, never using tobacco, never indulging in profane or rough language, always industrious and saving, and yet, as all men may see, he is dead at twenty-nine (God rest his manly soul), leaving me, his wife of six months, $3,000 worth of property. God forbid that I should curse his cowardly enemies, but they have appealed to the rope and by the rope they will finally perish—I predict it, for I know their crowding, overbearing spirit—let God forbid I should wish it. Men that have murdered the law can not appeal to the law.

I am reverently thankful that my poor boy, rushed suddenly into the presence of our Heavenly Father on that dark and fatal night by a merciless, Godless pack of cowards, did not appear at the Throne of Grace and mercy with the blood of any mortal dripping from his hands. I am done. I have only spoken because his dear lips are closed. I leave these men to the mercy of God and the punishment of their own conscience. Though the mill of justice be slow, it will grind their hearts to powder, as I believe, before they are on the limb.

My hands and the hands of my friends be clean of their blood, and God grant they may not be denied what they denied poor Ed. Watkins that cruel night—the the time to utter a prayer before they go to the presence of their God with their hands dripping with his innocent blood.

MRS. MARY F. WATKINS.

Carbonate Chronicle, September 8, 1883

Ranches for Sale in Aftermath

Despite her braves words of staying on the ranch, Mary Watkins sold the ranch property in 1884. She never returned to the Arkansas Valley.

A Bargain.

The finest stock range in the state of Colorado, known as the Watkins ranch, consisting of the s. ½ of the n. w. ¼ of section 25, township 50, n. of range 9 e N. M. M., containing 80 acres from 6 to 7 miles of good heavy log fence, a 2 story log house, nicely hewn, containing four rooms with a hallway between, cellar 12 x 14, good log stable with capacity for 6 horses, good stock corral, hennery, excellent spring, etc. Two acres under cultivation for a potato patch. The Sweet water range and Wells' gulch is included in the mountain pasture, the range is well watered. For further information apply to James F. Meagher, corner of F and Second streets.   3 24 tf

Salida Mail, March 29, 1884
Watkins Ranch Listing

A few months after the matter of Edwin Watkins concluded, William Gribble and A.J. Bates sold their cattle and land to the Mulock family. Perhaps the timing was coincidental, or maybe the transaction was planned for some time, but it is an odd occurrence at the least. It is proper to speculate that the two men wanted to get away from those who committed murder or may have been overwhelmed by their involvement.

> Mulock & Co., of Canon City, have purchased the herds of cattle owned by William M. Gribble and A. J. Bates and rights to range and water on what is known as South Park range, in Park, Fremont and Chaffee counties. The herds purchased aggregate about 2,000 head, and the price paid was $30 per head. Included in the purchase was the Bates ranch on Currant creek, with all the wagons and implements used thereon, and the Gribble ranch, on one fork of Badger creek, comprising several thousand acres of choice land under fence. This purchase added to the herd previously owned by Mulock & Co. swells the number to about 7,000 head. The brands transferred by Gribble are O. H. and J. K., and by Baltese a Maltese cross with A.V., below A. J. and an erect cross.

The Colorado Daily Chieftain, April 11, 1884

CHAPTER NINE

September 1883
Marshal Stingley First Encounters Frank Reed
—And Loses

Showdown at the Corral

By September 1883, Marshal Baxter Stingley was fully recovered from his earlier gunshot wounds and back on the job.

A week or so after the issuance of the warrant in Fremont County, Frank and Bent Jamison, two well-known cowboys, wandered into Salida one morning. Marshal Stingley met the men and advised them of the ordinance against having weapons in public. The duo decided to move on and headed to the stable to retrieve their horses.

After the warning, Stingley returned to his office and learned that a notice existed in Saguache County for Jamison's arrest. Stingley returned to the stable with his Deputy and found Frank Reed and Bent Jamison saddling their horses.

Stingley had experience dealing with desperate men, so he approached Jamison calmly, keeping both hands in his coat pockets. While appearing harmless, Stingley gripped his pistol. In the other pocket, he held the warrant.

When Marshal Stingley announced he intended to arrest the man, Jamison drew his gun and said, "I will never be taken alive."

Stingley thought about shooting Jamison with his hidden gun but looked over his shoulder and saw Frank Reed sitting on his horse with a rifle aimed at both the Marshal and the Deputy.

Frank Reed was an intimidating man, about 5'8 tall, 175 pounds, athletic with square shoulders, wide cheekbones, a dark complexion, and black eyes. The rifle probably made him appear even more menacing.

Baxter Stingley wisely backed down. He tried to appear calm and strolled outside the stable. Then he ran fast to his office for a shotgun and more deputies.

By the time the lawmen returned, Reed and Jamison were gone.

A DARING ACT.

Two Cow-Boys Stand-Off Marshal Stingley And Deputy Frizelle.

Yesterday morning two well-known cow-boys, named respectively Frank Reed and Bent Jamison, came into town, and paraded our streets, armed to the teeth. Our polite yet efficient city marshal, Baxter Stingley, mildly informed them that an ordinance prohibited the carrying of weapons in the city, and requested them to lay their arms aside. They promised to comply with this request, and about noon started toward the stable in the rear of Mrs. Fleck's restaurant, to get their horses and leave town. About this time a warrant was put into the hands of Marshal Stingley, by the sheriff of Saguache county, for the arrest of Bent Jamison, who is under indictment there. Knowing Jamison and Reed were about to leave town, Marshal Stingley hastily summoned his deputy, Mr. Frizelle, and went to where the men were getting their horses. Reed was already mounted, but Jamison was standing in the lot, near the stable door. Mr. Stingley approached him saying: "Bent, I have a warrant for you," at the same time having his hands in the pockets of a hunting coat—one on the warrant and the other on a small pistol. Jamison

the other on a small pistol. Jamison replied: "I will never be taken alive," drawing a forty-five. Stingley's first impulse was to shoot through his pocket; but, casting his eye over his shou'der, he discovered Reed, very near, with a cocked Winchester leveled on Frizelle and himself, and knew if he fired at Jamison, certain death awaited him, and, perhaps, his deputy as well. He continued talking to Jamison, and following him up, the latter backing toward the stable. Seeing no opportunity for either himself or his deputy to make a movement, Marshal Stingley left, and ran down the street for a shotgun and help; but the boy-boys were too quick for him, and hastily rode away.

Mountain Mail, September 15, 1883

They Meet Again

Following the issuance of a warrant for his arrest, Frank Reed regularly ventured into Salida, heavily armed, aching for a fight, and usually accompanied by Ernest Christison. Reed seems to have targeted Baxter Stingley for his anger.

On a Sunday evening in mid-October, the fugitives ran into the Marshal on First Street, outside the Windsor Hotel. The two had their pistols cocked and pointed and ordered Stingley to get off the street and go inside the hotel. The Marshal complied, making it twice Frank Reed had bested him.

officers. A week ago last Sunday night they met the marshal on the street in front of the Windsor hotel, and with cocked pistols compelled him to leave the street and enter the hotel. The next night they had a meeting with the marshal, who told them that he had no warrant for them and that he would not trouble them when they come to town if they would behave themselves. Christison said then "that he was willing to give up and go anywhere if he could have protection, but did not want to go to Buena Vista jail, as it was in charge of women, and he was afraid the same gang that hung Ed. Watkins would hang him." Frank Reed then said that he would never be taken alive. This ended the matter until last night

The Salida Daily News, October 29, 1883

From that moment on, locals said the sight of Reed had the same effect on Stingley as a red flag does on a bull. Stingley wanted nothing more than to arrest the man and put him away for a long time, but Reed was vicious and did not hesitate to use his gun, forcing Stingley to wait for the right moment.

Mutual friends, worried one or both might die, convinced Reed and Stingley to declare a truce and talk. Both men agreed to leave their guns in a boxcar for mutual safety before having a conversation. The meeting did not end well, with Stingley asserting he was the law and intended to arrest Reed the first chance he had. Christison spoke of his outstanding warrant in Canon City. He told the Marshal he was "willing to give up and go anywhere if he could have protection, but did not want to go to Buena Vista jail, as it was in charge of women, and he was afraid that the same gang that hung Edwin Watkins would hang him." Frank Reed told Stingley that he would never be taken alive because he would not get hanged by vigilantes.

This peace talk happened around October 20, 1883.

The feud between the two men finally became so bitter that finally, at the suggestion of friends, they met and had a consultation. In order that there should be no bloodshed, and to show that the intentions of all were peaceful, the men were disarmed, they leaving their revolvers in a box-car. The conference occurred about a week before the murder. It did not end as the friends of the principals had hoped. Stingley asserted that, as an officer of the law, he would arrest Reed when he saw a chance, upon the cattle-stealing indictment. He did not intend to spare him, no matter what his record was.

Denver Tribune, December 17, 1883

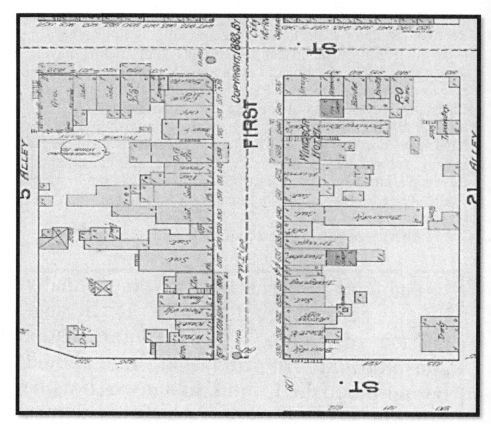

Sanborn Insurance Map of Salida, 1883
Library of Congress Archives
Windsor Hotel at top, near corner of First Street and F Street

time ago.

Reed was at one time employed by Watkins, his recklessness and daring making him a valuable acquisition to the corps of herders. He was feared by all the Watkins cowboys, and naturally their leader. Like nearly all others of his nature and disposition he was accused of cattle stealing, and as a conclusive proof of his guilt was found, the grand jury, at the first opportunity, found a true bill against him, and he became a fugitive from justice.

At the time of the Watkins lynching Reed appeared at Salida heavily armed and with the express determination of revenging the death of his former employer. No one thought of interfering with him, and no effort to capture him was made. He was feared because of his dangerous custom of using a revolver, and was held in great respect because of his mammoth proportions and his power as an athlete. He was, in a measure, the terror of the community.

About four weeks ago a man named Leni

Sioux City Journal, November 18, 1883

CHAPTER TEN

October 28, 1883
The Murder of Marshal Baxter Stingley

Baxter Stingley is announced by the Salida Mail as a republican candidate for sheriff subject to the decision of the convention.

Buena Vista Democrat, September 13, 1883

SALIDA, it seems, has a regularly organized band of thieves and burglars at work.—*Colorado Springs Republic.*

Yes, Salida has been infested with a gang of thieves and burglars, but the visits of this class of citizens are few and far between. Our police force, headed by our efficient marshal, Baxter Stingley, usually drop onto a gang as soon as they come to the city and their stay is short. Ornamenting the end of a rope has no charm in their eyes.

The Mountain Mail, October 30, 1883

Shootout

By 1883, Salida was known as "a live town—one full of 'life,' and possessing the glory of being 'bad,'" according to the *Denver Tribune*.

On October 28, Stingley returned from a Buena Vista train trip. As he exited the train, friends advised him that Frank Reed and Ernest Christison were inside the Arbour Dance Hall.

Around 8:30 p.m., Stingley walked inside the Arbour Dance Hall, located on First Street in Salida, beside the track just west of G Street. Entering the building, Stingley looked left and then right, where he saw the two bandits. Frank Reed leaned against the counter, hands in his coat pocket and talking to an old-time bartender George Triplett. The two had been speaking for several minutes. Ernest Christison stood beside Reed, drinking.

Reed looked up and saw the Marshal approaching but seemed unconcerned. He turned back to Triplett and continued chatting. Was Reed's attitude intentionally dismissive, based on his previous victories over Stingley? Or did Frank Reed have other plans for the Marshal? We can only speculate.

Marshal Baxter Stingley always carried two guns when on patrol. One pistol had an ivory handle with a bulldog pattern and a barrel made from blue steel. The other weapon was a silver-plated Colt .45. Stingley pulled the bulldog patterned gun out of the holster, holding it in his left hand, and walked across the saloon, directly towards Frank Reed. But the Marshal made a tactical error. He was an experienced gunman and knew he should leave space between him and Frank Reed, so Reed could not grab his gun or start a fight. Instead, Marshal Stingley walked up to Reed, laid the gun barrel against Reed's ribs, and said, "Frank, I have a warrant for you. Take your hands out of your pockets and throw them up."

Reed hesitated, said, "All right," and that is when all hell broke loose. Without warning, Reed's hands shot from his pockets, with one grabbing the barrel of Stingley's gun. His other hand clutched Stingley's arm.

The two men wrestled about ten feet from the bar. Reed snatched the gun from the Marshal, held it on the lawman, and fired.

Baxter Stingley threw up his left arm as if to block the shot. The bullet hit his wrist. Stingley balled up his shoulders and turned pale but quickly recovered and started toward Frank Reed.

Reed turned toward the rear door and fired at least two more times again. One bullet went through Stingley's arm and into his body, and another shot hit him in the leg.

Stingley stepped behind a post and pulled his second gun with his right hand when the third shot hit him. Now armed, Baxter Stingley stepped away from the pillar and started toward the rear door after Reed.

Some witnesses say he fired and hit the fleeing outlaw. Others said Stingley was finished, and his shot hit the ceiling.

Regardless, Frank Reed ducked out the alley door and ran.

The Marshal did not give chase. Instead, he stood in the doorway, his legs wobbling, his world swirling around him.

Mr. Arbour, the owner of the saloon, asked Stingley if he was hurt.

"Yes," Stingley said. "He shot me three times."

Mr. Arbour and a few patrons grabbed Stingley and laid him on a table. They pulled off his boots for comfort and were shocked to see both had already filled with blood.

Patrons carried Stingley into the anteroom, and Dr. Underhill arrived quickly. The leg wound was nothing serious, but the shot to the side soon proved fatal. The doctor could not locate the slug for removal.

Citizens rushed to the saloon and attempted to comfort the Marshal. Mr. Arbour brought in a mattress and coverings and had the music and dancing stopped. He kept the business as quiet as possible.

Baxter Stingley knew the end was near and said to a friend, Harry Hakins, "Harry, I don't want to die in a dance house." His final words were, "I made a mistake getting so close to him."

By midnight, Stingley began sinking and died around three in the morning. He was 38 and served as the Marshal of Salida for exactly two years.

A postmortem indicated the missing bullet found a home in Stingley's left kidney. The bullet did not hit any bone but was battered, indicating it was probably the shot that first struck Baxter in the wrist.

~

death.

It was at his own request that the post mortem was made.

While H. J. Hakins was holding him up during the examination of his wounds he whispered, "Harry, I don't want to die in a dance house."

His last words were "I made a mistake in getting so close to him."

The Salida Daily News, October 29, 1883

The nation was stunned by Marshal Baxter Stingley's murder, which made every major newspaper, including *The New York Times*.

The entire State of Colorado was shocked and outraged.

Colorado Governor Grant issued a $1,000 reward for the capture of Frank Reed, dead or alive, and Chaffee County offered the same amount. The City of Salida posted a $500 bonus. In today's dollars, the reward totaled around $100,000.

~

The 1880s were a rough time to be alive, and life was cheap by any measure. As if to illustrate that truth, two weeks after Stingley's murder, partygoers laughed and danced and drank and chased girls at the Arbour Dance Hall, seemingly oblivious to the enormous bloodstain beneath their feet—the last mark of Marshal Baxter Stingley.

Arbour Dance Hall
From *Over Trails of Yesterday, Book One*

IN MEMORIAM.

WHEREAS, It has pleased the Divine Ruler of the Universe to remove from our midst while at his post of duty, our dearly beloved brother, Baxter Stingley, thereby causing us to mourn the loss of one who, as a member of this lodge has always been true and faithful in the discharge of his duties, and whose daily life and walk was a living example of the true knight, always brave in defending the right, and equally courageous in prosecuting the wrong, and

WHEREAS, by the untimely death of Brother Stingley this lodge has met with irreparable loss, he being one of its most earnest and faithful members; Salida and Chaffee county, one of its most useful citizens, and humanity one of its noblest defenders, yet we humbly bow to the mandates of him who doeth all things well, and hope that what is our loss will be His gain.

The Mountain Mail, November 3, 1883

Funeral

The citizens of Salida were devastated by Stingley's murder. Despite connections to criminals and possibly illegal activity, Baxter Stingley was an outstanding Marshal. Crime had become rare rather than commonplace, and the town was rid of the trash, stray animals, and deadbeats.

City officials closed the town on the day of Stingley's funeral, and flags lowered to half-mast.

In the days before the memorial service, every train arriving in Salida overflowed with mourners. On the morning of the service, streets filled early, as everyone wanted to pay respects to the slain lawman. More than 3,000 people attended Baxter Stingley's funeral—the largest ever in Chaffee County.

The Knights of Pythias, a fraternity, handled the service. They formed in front of the town hall, marched to the undertakers, and escorted Stingley's remains. During the procession, the city band and the fire company joined the fraternity members, and the group arrived at the Craig Opera House at 11 a.m.

In the eulogy, a Reverend noted Stingley's dedication to duty and the fact he never shrank from danger.

Following a public viewing of the body, a mile-long procession walked three miles to the Cleora Cemetery, where the band played Baxter's favorite song, bringing tears to the eyes of many. The Knights of Pythias and the fire company circled Stingley's grave and performed a ceremony.

The funeral of Marshal Stingley which occurred here to-day, was the largest ever held in this county, fully three thousand persons being present.

Leadville Daily Herald, November 1, 1883

Knights of Pythias funeral procession for Marshal Baxter Stingley, 1883

CHAPTER ELEVEN

October 1883
Murderer Frank Reed Disappears

Murderer Wanted.

Sheriff W. W. Strait was in receipt of the following letter yesterday from the Sheriff of Chaffee county :

BUENA VISTA, October 29. — Sheriff Strait: Look out for Frank Reed, about five feet eight, dark complexion, black eyes, wide cheek bones, very short chin, square shoulders, weight 175 pounds, re ported wounded. Hold for murder of Baxter Stingley, deputy shot at Salida.

ROBERT RAY, Sheriff.

Baxter Stingley, the murdered man, was marshal of Salida, and the murderer, Frank Reed, is a Chaffee county cowboy. Stingley held a warrant for his arrest and went into a Salida dance hall to arrest his man. Reed resisted arrest and shot Stingley three times, and it is thought was himself shot once by the marshal. Reed then escaped and has not since been heard from. Our latest report last night stated that Stingley was not dead, but could not possibly live.

The Colorado Daily Chieftain, October 30, 1883

Escape

Immediately, Frank Reed vanished without a trace, a tricky accomplishment considering every law enforcement officer in the State and every detective hungry for a considerable reward were part of the search.

Rumors abounded as to his whereabouts.

One reasonable report was that Reed hid for a while at the ranch of his friend, Ernest Christison. Reed was also seen after midnight in a Salida saloon the Saturday after the shooting. He begged a drink from the bartender, chatted for a bit, then left. Unreliable rumors discussed Frank Reed returning to Salida multiple times, accompanied by three or four hardened men, but these accounts appear to be fabrications.

To escape a county-wide chase required a lot of assistance, especially considering that witnesses to the murder claimed Reed received a gunshot wound from Marshal Stingley.

> It is claimed that Frank Reed was seen at Christison's ranch, Thursday.

Buena Vista Democrat, November 29, 1883

of a $3,200 reward. The officers had been informed that Reed had been in the habit of going into Salida every Saturday night since the killing, for the purpose of getting drunk and having a good time with the painted beauties who ornament the dance halls. The informant stated that he always had three or four friends with him who were determined men, and that he openly defied the authorities. When the information was sifted down it was found to be greatly exaggerated. Reed had come into town only once since the killing and he was alone. He rode in quietly after midnight and going to the back door of a saloon begged a drink. The barkeeper was the only man who saw him and they only exchanged a few words. Since that time Reed has not been seen and all efforts to hunt him have been abandoned as it is pretty well assured that he has left the country. The

Carbonate Chronicle, December 15, 1883

November 1883

Ernest Christison was arrested the following month while driving stolen cattle from Watkins ranch to St. Elmo. Christison served seven years in prison for the crime.

Lack of Coverage

Newspaper reporting in 1883 involved little investigation and was often overt in bias, openly supporting those with whom they agreed politically and vocally opposed to those on the other side.

A few things are curious about the local newspaper coverage of Stingley's murder and Reed's escape. First, there was never any reporting of the hunt for Frank Reed or speculation about how he vanished or who helped him. For other stories, such as the murder of Edwin Watkins, the newspaper voiced endless opinions and named suspects. *The Mountain Mail* wrote sixteen stories about Watkins within six months of his murder. But for Baxter Stingley's killing? Only two articles came out after the initial day-after coverage.

There were also no articles about the escape of Frank Reed— no speculation, no follow-up. And unlike other newspapers around the State, local editors gave minimal coverage of suspected sightings and arrests of men thought to be Reed. The newspaper appeared to be influenced, but by what or whom we will probably never know.

Indications of Conspiracy

One obscure article mentioned Frank Reed working for the cattlemen who lynched Edwin Watkins. This theory said Frank Reed murdered Baxter Stingley for money, to shut him up and ensure he could not carry out his threats of revenge for the lynching of his friend. Baxter Stingley was the last man connected to the theft operation—Watkins was dead, Thomas Cameron closed the meat market, Jesse Stingley and Roe Cameron raced out of town, and the other peripheral members were arrested. Stingley was the only one left who could harm the murderous cattle organization.

Little else explains what happened to Reed in the aftermath, and the theory of Reed as a paid assassin makes considerable sense.

Following the lynching of Edwin Watkins, Frank Reed repeatedly appeared in Salida and attempted to force a confrontation with Marshal Stingley. First was the incident at the corral, followed by pulling a gun on the Marshal outside the Windsor Hotel. Even the peace conference ended contentiously. Frank Reed never attempted to hide from the law in Salida despite an outstanding warrant for cattle theft in Fremont County. He continuously provoked Stingley, if only by walking the streets, as if to create a situation where gunplay could be justified.

Alternatively, Frank Reed simply did not see Baxter Stingley as a threat and dismissed the man despite the badge on his chest. But with a cattle theft warrant hanging over his head, it looks unlikely Frank Reed would be so careless unless he were unconcerned about prosecution.

If the murder was premeditated, then powerful and wealthy men were behind the killing of Baxter Stingley. And there is much to contemplate with this hypothesis.

Stingley's open alignment with Edwin Watkins during the cattlemen's trial in Salida made him a threat and a target. At a minimum, Stingley had turned a blind eye to the criminal activities of Watkins, Christison, Cameron, and his brother, Jesse. When he swore revenge against those who murdered his friend, Stingley appears to have created enemies unafraid of homicide. As written in their public letter, the cattlemen viewed the killing of thieves as justifiable and held no shame or sorrow for their murderous deed.

If left alive, Marshal Stingley would have had the power and determination to investigate Watkins's murder (Edwin Watkins was, after all, a citizen of Salida) and held enough influence to force a prosecution.

One thing is sure—Frank Reed did not drop off the face of the earth without assistance.

A HEAVY REWARD.

Governor Grant Offers One Thousand Dollars for the Arrest of the Salida Murderer.

Governor Grant has issued a reward of $1,000 for the apprehension of Frank Reed, the murderer of Baxter Stingley, of Salida. At a recent mass meeting held in Salida resolutions were passed denouncing the murder, and a petition signed by the most prominent citizens of Salida was forwarded to the Governor, asking that a reward of $1,000 be given for Reed's arrest. The petition sets forth that Reed is a desperado and is shielded by a set of cattle thieves, and for that reason a large reward was asked. The petition also asked Governor Grant to give a reward for the body of Reed, either dead or alive, but the governor refused to give a reward, except for the arrest of the murderer. The following is the reward:

REWARD FOR FRANK REED.

STATE OF COLORADO,
GOVERNOR'S OFFICE,
DENVER, November 3, 1883.

It being represented to me that Baxter Stingley, the marshal of the town of Salida, and a deputy sheriff of Chaffee county, was, on the night of the twenty-eighth of October, 1883, murdered by one Frank Reed; and

WHEREAS, It is represented that said Frank Reed is a noted outlaw and desperado, and that said murder was committed in a felonious and premeditated manner, while the said Baxter Stingley was in the discharge of his duty, in making the arrest of the said Frank Reed; and

WHEREAS, Said Reed has escaped, and successfully eludes the officers of said county in effecting his arrest and capture; and

WHEREAS, the mayor of Salida has offered a reward of $1,000 for his arrest; and

WHEREAS, I am petitioned by a large number of the citizens of said county to offer an additional reward of $1,000, now,

Therefore, I, James B. Grant, governor of the state of Colorado, do hereby offer a reward of $1,000 for the arrest and delivery of the said. Reed to the proper authorities of said county of Chaffee.   JAMES B. GRANT, Governor.

Leadville Daily Herald, November 6, 1883

Covering Tracks

Two months after Stingley's murder, the South Park stock raisers (Park County) met and decided to offer a reward for the capture of Frank Reed. They put up over $500 ($10,000 today). The committee agreeing on this action included J.R. Witcher and Edward Mulock, men who Marshal Baxter Stingley and Deputy Sheriff Miles Mix threatened and intimidated in August. These men were also part of the group suspected of murdering Edwin Watkins.

FIELD NOTES.

Meeting of Stock Men at Kester.--An Increased Reward for Frank Reed.

A meeting of South Park stock raisers was held at Kester in this county on Saturday the 1st inst. From W. R. Smith and others we gather the following report: The proper officers of the stock association not being present, W. H. Beery called the meeting to order. S. C. Haver, of the Cleveland Cattle company, was elected a member of the association and was also installed secretary for the occasion.

On motion it was determined to offer an additional reward of $500 for the arrest of Frank Reed, the murderer of city marshal Baxter Stingley, of Salida, and a notorious cattle thief. The committee named to collect this amount from members of the association consists of W. H. Beery, J. R. Witcher, E. P. Mulock, W. R. Smith, T. H. Robbins and Rob't Fester. The committee was instructed to deposit the full amount with Mr. Mulock. From the liberal amounts pledged for that purpose it is believed the total will exceed $500 considerably.

The Fairplay Flume, December 13, 1883

1884—Rumored Sightings

Despite a considerable reward, Frank Reed disappeared. Unofficial sightings of the murderer were widespread and had him living everywhere from Illinois to Pennsylvania to Arizona.

One detective claimed to have come across Reed working as a cowboy in Arizona but said he was too frightened to arrest the man, as Reed was considered vicious even by 1883 standards. It appears the law was afraid of Frank Reed.

Based on their actions over the next few years, many influential people in Salida and Chaffee County also seemed frightened of Frank Reed or were fearful of what he would say if brought to trial.

Yesterday's Denver *Tribune* gives an account of the arrest of Frank Reid, the slayer of our brave marshal, Baxter Stingley, at Winona, Ill., September 6, by the sheriff of that p'ace, on an order fom the Rocky Mountain Detective Assoc'ation. He will be returned to Colorado at once, a requisition having already been sent to Illinois. This news will be received by our citizens with rejoicing, and we only hope that it is the right Frank Reid, then the state authorities and stock association will not hesitate to pay the reward to the sheriff of Winona, justly due him. Once here, we hope that he will get the benefit of the full extent of the law.

Salida Mail, March 15, 1884

MR. REED THE COWBOY.

Marshal Stingley's Murderer Said to Be Punching Cows in Arizona.

A Fine Chance to Get a Reputation and Make Some Money at the Same Time.

Leadville Daily Herald, August 7, 1884

It is said Frank Reed the murderer of Baxter Stingly has been captured in Illinois.

Buena Vista Democrat, August 21, 1884

1885—Curious Refusal

A Frank Reed, one seemingly connected to crime in Salida, was arrested in 1885 in Birmingham, Alabama. While the official report was that the man in Alabama was not the same Frank Reed wanted in Colorado, Salida did not send anyone to confirm his identity and, in fact, refused to pay for the prisoner's extradition. City officials also declined to pay the reward money even if the man was the same Frank Reed. Odder still, this Frank Reed allegedly confessed to murdering a man in Salida and said he stole more cattle than "he knew what to do with."

Capture of Frank Reed.

Special to Daily Review-Press.

SALIDA, August 20.—A telegram received here to-day verifies the report as telegraphed the REVIEW-PRESS yesterday of the capture of Frank Reed, the slayer of Marshall Baxter Stingley, October 28, 1883. There was a reward of $4,000 offered for Reed's apprehension. He was captured in Birmingham, Alabama, and will be brought back to Colorado on a requisition from the Governor, which will be applied for to-day.

Gunnison Review-Press, August 22, 1885

The man arrested and suspected to be Frank Reed the murderer of Baxter Stingley, turns out not to be Frank Reed after all.

Buena Vista Democrat, September 9, 1885

A Notorious Criminal.

NEW YORK, August 18.—The Herald's Birmingham, Ala., special says: Frank Reed an alleged notorious California criminal, was arrested Sunday at Sileria. Reed came here a year ago with his wife and two children. A detective worked up the case and kept up with his man by acting the role of carpenter and lumberman, and thus managing to get enough of his confidence to warrant his arresting him. The prisoner when arrested said. "I know what it is for. I know it is about a cattle matter in the West. I'm the guilty man." He even confesses that he killed a man in Salida, Colo., and a woman in a Texas bagnio, besides stealing more cattle than he knew what to do with. The chief of police of Salida was telegraphed to send a man to identify Reed.

Gunnison Press-Review, August 22, 1885

April 1887—Another Credible Arrest

A very credible arrest happened in 1887 in Pennsylvania.

This man was named Frank Wells, but the law presumed him to be the wanted criminal Frank Reed. Wells worked as a brickmaker (as did the Salida Frank Reed) and had a peculiar triangular scar above his left eye (as did the man wanted in Salida). He was about the same age and the same height and weight. When not punching cattle, the Frank Reed of Salida made bricks for Mix and Company (owned by Deputy Sheriff Miles Mix) as late as 1882.

> The principle cause of this murder dates two years back, and possibly more. Frank Reed the murderer, worked at that time in Mix & Co's brick yard: the cattle thieving in this county had been notorious; it was known to every person, residents of the county who the cattle thieves were, and to this hour the posted men of the city are cognizant of the facts, rumors and interpretations of words used that caused the murder.

Buena Vista Democrat, November 1, 1883

Frank Reed—1883 and 1887

Compare two descriptions, one of Frank Reed in December 1883, the other of Frank Wallace, possibly Frank Reed, in Pennsylvania in April 1887.

	1883	1887
Weight	170-180 pounds	170 pounds
Age	About 24-25	About 33
Scar	Above left eye	Above left eye
Occupation	Brick maker (1882)	Brick maker

Salida's Killer Thought to Be Captured in Pennsylvania.

GLENSBURG, Pa., April 28.—Detectives arrested Frank Wells at Black Lick, Indiana county, last night, charged with murder.

Wells is supposed to be Frank Reed, who is charged with the murder of City Marshal Stingley, of Salida, Colorado, on October 28, 1880. Nothing has been heard of him since the murder. Several months ago he was finally located at Black Lick, where he followed the occupation of a brick maker, and his identity was discovered by means of a peculiar triangular scar above his left eye. One thousand dollars was offered for his body dead or alive. He is married, aged about 33 years, and weighs about 170 pounds.

Wells says that he is innocent, and thinks that he is the victim of a practical joke.

Colorado Daily Chieftain, April 29, 1887

A circular has been issued by Mayor Westerfield, of Salida, offering rewards aggregating $3,500 for the arrest and delivery to the sheriff of Chaffee county of one Frank Reed, the murderer of Marshal Stingley of Salida. The man who captures the murderer will certainly be in luck. He is described as follows: Height, five feet eight or nine inches; complexion dark; weight 170 to 180; eyes, black or dark brown; when last seen had a short dark moustache, dark brown hair, cut short; nice teeth, stout and regular; large mouth; thin lips; short chin; bull-dog expression of countenance; a plain scar on forehead, over one eye; age twenty-four or twenty-five years; when last seen had on a light-colored, broad-brimmed hat with fair leather band; former occupation, blacksmith, for the last year has been a cow-boy, and prides himself as such; is an athlete and drinks considerably; when drinking is quarrelsome and boisterous.

The original description of Frank Reed, December 7, 1883.

Frank Reed, who killed Marshal Stingley of Salida, in October last, has been captured in Pennsylvania sailing under the name of Frank Wells.

Gunnison Review-Press, April 30, 1887

The thorny path of the fugitive from justice is well exampled in the case of Frank Reed, who shot City Marshal Baxter Stingley, of Salida, on October 25, 1885, in Black Lick, Pennsylvania. Reed, who used to be a gay and happy cowboy in Colorado, was found working in a brick-yard when apprehended.

Buena Vista Democrat, May 5, 1887

May 1887—Rewards Withdrawn

      Not only did Salida officials again refuse to send someone to confirm the identity of the man in Pennsylvania or pay for the extradition, but several days later, they passed a special ordinance withdrawing all reward money for the capture of Frank Reed. The State of Colorado soon followed, taking back their reward offer.

A resolution withdrawing rewards offered by the town of Salida for the arrest of Frank Reed, was adopted.

Salida Mail, May 6, 1887

1893—Chastised by Police

A final credible claim of Frank Reed's arrest occurred in 1893 in Brazil, Indiana. But once again, the Salida city council said 'no' to paying for his return, prompting an Officer to blast the city. "I doubt if any reward will be paid," said the Indiana sheriff who arrested Frank Reed. "As the officials refused then (he was referring to the past arrests), I suppose they will do nothing in the matter now."

DENVER, Jan. 21.—The following telegram was received by the chief of police from Brazil, Ind., yesterday:

Send exact description of Frank Reid, giving full particulars of case. Is reward good? Answer at once. I have a man located that fills description.

LEVI LOUDERBACK,
Chief of Police.

Reid is the man who killed Baxter Stingley, marshal of Salida, who attempted to arrest him on October 28, 1883, for horse stealing. He escaped and a reward of $1,000 was offered for his apprehension at that time, $500 of which was to be paid by the state and the balance by the county. Reid was afterward heard of in Texas while he was with a circus, but the state had withdrawn its reward and the officials allowed him to go.

Salida Mail, January 24, 1893

CHAPTER TWELVE

Who Was Frank Reed?

A Chapter of Investigative Speculation

Frank Reed did not magically disappear; he was just never found. Somewhere, a man who once used the name Frank Reed continued living. This chapter asks 'what if' and 'where.' Perhaps we will never solve the mystery of Frank Reed, but it is worth exploring possibilities.

Reed was an oddity—appearing in the Arkansas Valley out of nowhere around 1882 before returning to the ether a year later. No records exist of him outside of his brief time in Salida.

A deep examination points to the possibility, perhaps probability, that Reed was a career criminal who changed names as often as his location.

At a minimum, the path laid out here is credible and worth considering.

Frank Reed was a killer—that is a fact. He was a thief—that also is undeniable. And he regularly appears connected to corrupt officials and criminal enterprises, particularly cattle theft.

Who was Frank Reed? We will probably never know. Countless men had the name Frank Reed, and most likely none examined here are the murderer from Salida, but a few stand out and are worth considering.

April 1875

The first time a criminal named Frank Reed appears in Colorado records was April 1875.

The New York Times wrote a lengthy article, reprinted in *The Rocky Mountain News*, about George Van Velsor, a railway clerk arrested for a series of crimes in New York.

In May 1874, Van Velsor stole $33,000 from the New York Central and Hudson Railroad, worth around $750,000 today. He had an accomplice in the robbery, but the two divided up the money and parted ways.

Van Velsor ran with his share of the stolen funds to Denver, Colorado, where he lived fast, and spent huge sums under the name of Frank Reed. A saloon keeper, supposedly taken into Reed's confidence, betrayed Reed and turned him into a local sheriff after the man calling himself Frank Reed refused to pay hush money to keep the secret.

When arrested, Van Velsor had nearly $200,000 cash on his person (in modern worth) along with a gold watch, $5,000 in gold (today's value), and a revolver.

The Denver Sheriff allegedly offered a deal—turn over all the money, and Reed could 'escape.' Reed rejected the proposal. When released to New York police, the Denver officer handed over the watch, gold, and gun but refused to release the money.

George Van Velsor (Frank Reed) was convicted in June 1875 and sentenced to four years in Sing Sing State Prison prison. He was released on September 28, 1878, after the removal of one year of his sentence for good behavior.

Van Velsor's partner in crime was also caught and convicted.

George Van Velsor disappeared from public records after his pardon.

three weeks ago, when Superintendent Walling received a dispatch from Sheriff Willoughby, of Denver City, Colorado, informing him that he was on the track of a young man calling himself Frank Reed, but who was supposed to be Van Velsor. He was living a fast life, spending money freely, and said that he had been sojourning in Southern Kansas for several months. Superintendent Wal-

fugitives, were sent all through the country. One of these circulars found its way into the hands of Sheriff Willoughby, and he has been on the lookout for the fugitives ever since. About three weeks ago a young man arrived in Denver from the East, and went south toward Puebla. In about ten days he returned to Denver. He was soon after arrested and identified as Van Velsor.

The New York Times, March 26, 1875

The Story He Told the Officials in that City About the Officials of This.

The New York *Times* of Monday contains the following account of the arrival at the metropolis of Van Velsor, the defaulting railway clerk recently arrested in this city, with the accompanying epitome of his adventures.

Officer Shelly, of the Nineteenth sub-precinct, arrived at the Grand Central depot at an early hour Saturday morning, having in custody George Van Velsor, the clerk who, in May last, stole $33,000 in greenbacks from the office of the treasurer of the New York Central & Hudson River railroad, and who was arrested by the sheriff of Denver City, Colorado, about two weeks ago. A history of the crime and the details of Van Velsor's arrest were published in the *Times* of Friday. On arriving at the depot Van Velsor was met by his mother and sister, and the meeting was very affecting. The prisoner was subsequently brought to police headquarters, and on being arraigned before Superintendent Walling, seemed to feel his disgraceful position most keenly. After remaining a short time at the central office, Van Velsor was taken to the office of the District Attorney, and from thence committed to the Tombs to await trial. Van Velsor gives a graphic account of the adventures of himself and his companion, Isaac Baxter, after leaving New York. On reaching maryland they buried $18,000 in old newspapers and their clothing, donned second-hand suits purchased in New York, and traveled to Indianapolis, Quincy, Ill., Kansas City, and Southern Kansas, where they purchased a ranch for $500 and went to farming. After settling down they returned to Maryland on the 8th of July and dug up the buried treasure, $2,000 of which, having been injured by the damp, they burned. After five months' illness Van Velsor divided the spoils with Baxter and the latter disappeared. Van Velsor, in the middle of February, left his ranch and went to Denver, Col., where he led a fast life under the name of Frank Reed, spent large sums of money, and was betrayed to a New York Deputy Sheriff by a saloon-keeper named Schoaf, after the latter had failed to extort any more money from him. He was then arrested by Sheriff Willoughby on a charge of carrying concealed weapons, and that officer telegraphed the fact to New York. The Sheriff took possession of $1,660 in gold, and a gold watch and chain and a revolver, found on Van Velser's person, and $7,000 in greenbacks found in his trunk. Van Velser states that the sheriff offered to "fix" the affair and let him off before the arrival of the New York officers, but that he refused to accept the offer, having all along expressed his willingness to surrender to the officers of the law and bear the punishment of his crime. He afterward sent Schoaf to the prisoner with a paper signing over $5,000 to him, and subsequently a lawyer offered to get him out for $1,000, both of which offers he refused. Sheriff Willoughby subsequently offered him $3,000 if he would quit Colorado, leaving the remainder of the money in his hands. This offer he also refused, and was then allowed every opportunity to escape from the sheriff's house, where he had been removed from the jail, but declined to do so. Finally, he says, he was handed over to the New York detectives, Shelly and Scanlan, who demanded his property from the sheriff. That official did surrender the jewelry and clothing, but refused to give up the money, saying that Vanderbilt was rich and could bear the loss. Steps will immediately be taken to compel the Colorado sheriff to disgorge his stealings.

In reference to the above, Mr. Willoughby assures a reporter of THE NEWS that he had taken legal advice as to his action, and was ready to abide by the result. As the New York folk take legal action in the matter, the upshot of it all can hardly fail to clear Willoughby's skirts entirely, or do decidedly the other thing; there wont be much half way work about it.

The Rocky Mountain News, April 7, 1875

STATE OF NEW YORK.

Executive Chamber.

Albany, Sept. 28, 1878.

The Secretary of State is requested to make out a **Restoration to the Rights of Citizenship** for *George Van Velsor* who was convicted of *Grand Larceny* in the County of *New York* in the month of *June* 1875 and was sentenced to *the Sing Sing State Prison, Transferred to Auburn for the term of four years, which term he served subject to the legal deduction for good conduct.*

L. Robinson

New York, U.S., Executive Orders for Commutations, Pardons, Restorations, Clemency, and Respites 1845-1931

April 1882

Four years after George Van Velsor, aka Frank Reed of Denver, was pardoned, a Frank Reed appeared in Colorado. He was arrested for assault and robbery in Las Animas (roughly 175 miles from Salida). That same year, Frank Reed, the murderer of Baxter Stingley, arrived in Salida, working cattle and making bricks for Miles Mix.

Are these two men the same person? That cannot be determined, but circumstantial evidence and geographic closeness point to it being a distinct probability.

People vs. Frank Reed and Wm. Rogers; robbery. Found guilty of assault. Uriel Robinson defendants' attorney.

Las Animas Leader, April 14, 1882

July 1892—Arrested in Idaho

After his murderous crime spree in Salida, claims of finding 'the' Frank Reed popped up across the county, as discussed in the previous chapter. One such Reed was arrested for murder in 1892 near Wallace, Idaho. A military detachment was sent to secure his arrest and protect Reed from lynchers.

WALLACE, July 17.—The western part of Wallace at the mouth of the placid creek is now a tented field. Eight companies of troops arrived from Fort Keogh, Montana, to-day and will be distributed in various portions of the mining district. The entire command here was suddenly called to arms at 11 o'clock to search the neighboring hills in the hope of capturing the miners who have been in hiding. Six were arrested. Many of the miners under arrest are married and have families, and to-day many wives and children were seen about the camp seeking the privilege of speaking to the head of the family who is held prisoner. In most instances this privilege was granted.

It is probable the entire body of miners under arrest will be tried in the United States district court for contempt, though some will have to answer to a charge of murder. A detachment of troops went to Murray to-day and brought Frank Reed, the murderer of R. W. Stevens, to Wallace for safe keeping, as threats of lynching were heard on all sides and a well organized mob had planned to attack the jail to-night

The Aspen Daily Times, July 18, 1892

November 1893—Death in Chicago

While there is nothing definitive connecting the men, a Frank Reed of Denver died in a train accident in Chicago. The fact that George Van Velsor used the name of Frank Reed while living in Denver is intriguing if nothing else.

Denver Man Killed.

CHICAGO, Nov. 14.—Frank Reed, from Denver, supposed to be a laboring man, was killed by an Illinois Central passenger train. He was trying to avoid one train and was struck by a second train which he did not see.

The Aspen Daily Chronicle, November 14, 1893

July 1899—Frank Wallace

Rumors in Colorado said Frank Reed changed his name to Frank Wallace and continued a life of crime.

One Frank Wallace committed suicide in jail in Missouri in July 1899. Before leaping 100 feet from a staircase to his death, Wallace left behind a letter addressed to his sister in Canon City, Colorado. Canon City is in Fremont County, where Frank Reed conducted most of his known cattle thefts with Edwin Watkins and Ernest Christison.

Jefferson City, Mo. July 24.—Convict Frank Wallace of Kansas City committed suicide this morning by jumping from the topmost step of the stairway of the clothing department to the pavement, a distance of 100 feet. He died instantly. He left a letter addressed to his sister, living in Cañon City, Colorado, telling her that he had lost all hope of securing his liberty, and concluded by saying that suicide was the only course for relief from misery. The prison officials refuse to disclose the sister's name.

The Canon City Record, July 27, 1899

CHAPTER THIRTEEN

Tying Up Loose Ends

Success of the Ranching Syndicate

It is undeniable that a known group of influential and wealthy ranchers started a movement to eliminate the cattle theft ring that reduced their herds and income. When reviewing those whom this group targeted, the cattlemen's triumph is evident.

- Jesse Hooper Stingley left Colorado in March 1883 and did not return until 1895. He did not return to Salida until 1893.

- Roe Cameron left the State in March 1883 and did not return until 1900.

- Edwin Watkins was murdered in August 1883.

- Thomas Cameron closed his meat market in September 1883.

- Marshal Baxter Stingley was murdered on October 28, 1883.

- Ernest Christison was convicted for cattle theft, 1884 and served seven years in jail.

- Frank Reed disappeared forever.

- Mr. Fuller, Charlie Christison, John C. Myers, Billy Taylor, and John Taylor were arrested as members of the theft ring, but no record was found of the outcome.

- Miles Mix resigned as Chaffee County Constable in March 1884 and moved to Missoula, Montana.

> The resignation of Miles Mix as constable of precinct No. 16 was received and acceptad. It is ordered that Al Ryan be appointeg to fill vacancy.

Buena Vista Democrat, March 6, 1884

T. Witcher

The man who filed charges against Edwin Watkins for cattle theft, the same rancher Mary Watkins successfully sued for stealing her husband's cattle and claiming them as his own in court, became one of the region's most prosperous cattlemen. He unsuccessfully ran for county commissioner in 1901. In 1908, he sold his cattle, around 3,000 head in total, and retired. A decade later, Witcher's son was elected District Attorney for the Eleventh Judicial District, which covers Park, Fremont, Custer, and Chaffee counties.

> One of the biggest live stock deals consummated in the county for a long time was the sale a few days ago by T. Witcher of Cotopaxi, of all of his cattle, numbering between two and three thousand head to Samuel Pepper and associates of Denver. The transaction was brought about through the agency of Charley Halsey of Pueblo, who, it is understood, will receive 50 cents a head upon all of the cattle involved in the trade. The cattle of the Witcher brand range from Cotopaxi northward along the slopes of the continental divide as far as the Stirrup ranch, on the borders of Park county. It is stated that Mr. Witcher will permanently retire from the cattle business.

The Canon City Record, February 27, 1909

The Mulock Clan

The empire of Ira Mulock and his sons crashed in 1888 after their bank failed when the institutional debts far exceeded the deposits. Ira and his brother, Joshua, were indicted on larceny charges and faced countless civil lawsuits. A woman who lost everything in the scandal attacked Ira on the street of Canon City with a horsewhip. He responded by choking and beating the woman until passersby pulled him off. Ira soon fled to Mexico and remained there until he died in 1893 at the age of 61. Edson Mulock was in Leadville by 1900, Peter Mulock moved to Chaffee County, and Parker Mulock spent the rest of his life raising cattle in Texas.

> Indictments have been found in the Fremont county District court against A. R. Gumaer, Ira Mulock and Joshua Mulock. Also by civil process a great many judgments have been entered up against them.

The Fairplay Flume, April 12, 1888

> Ira Mulock is kept in hot water perpetually by the creditors of the defunct Exchange bank. Many of them do not hesitate to say that he willfully robbed them. He has been arrested so many times that he now finds great difficulty in giving bonds.

The Fairplay Flume, May 31, 1888

The Woman Whacked Him.

Intense excitement was created at Canon City Saturday, and in was but a second until a dense crowd had collected in front of the McClure house. Ann Murray, a poor laundress, honest and hard-working, had deposited in the late rotton Exchange bank, which failed there recently, $200 of her own money and $90 for a poor working girl named Rose Gallagher. This money was earned by these poor women by extremely hard work, and they claim that the Mulocks have robbed them. Meeting Ira Mulock on the sidewalk Ann Murray threw a large quantity of red pepper in his eyes, and followed it up by clubbing him over the head with a heavy, square hickory club three feet long which she had shrewdly concealed in an oil cloth cover to represent an umbrella, so that her intention might not be detected.

As soon as Mulock recovered from his awkward predicament and surprise, he grappled with her and began choking and striking her with his fists.

A large crowd soon rushed in and prevented him from punishing her. He called her many vile names and she swears revenge for that also. Mulock was rushed out of sight in the hotel, and was later taken to his home by two protectors.

A purse was raised by the citizens to have the brass band serenade Ann Murray that evening.

Salida Mail, May 15, 1888

The death of Ira Mulock is now announced and this time we think it is a correct report. Once before the report was out that he had died, but it was found that he was only in very poor health. He died at Aquas Calientas, in Old Mexico, at the age of sixty-one years.

The Fairplay Flume, February 9, 1893

Thomas Ninemeyer

Following his arrest for murdering Deputy Sheriff James Bathurst and the railroad employee J.D. Gannon, Thomas Ninemeyer, along with ten others, broke out of the Chaffee County jail during a fire January 1884. Ninemeyer visited his mother after the jail escape, then disappeared forever.

> It is authoritively stated that the murderer, Ninemeyer, after his escape from jail at Buena Vista, visited his mother near this place and partook of breakfast; also that he was visited by a number of friends who offered him arms and such other aid as he desired. He turned the horse that was given him at the time of escape loose at this point, and remarked to his mother: "They may capture the others, but they will never take me me alive!"

Salida Mail, February 23, 1884

Ernest Virgil Christison

Ernest Christison escaped jail with Ninemeyer and nine others in 1884. He. was found hiding in the barn of Thomas Cameron, the father of Jesse Stingley's wife. After serving his prison sentence, Christison was released in 1891 at the age of 39. He gave up the life of crime, married, had children, and lived out his days near Salida as a farmer raising oats, hay, and potatoes. In the off-season, he worked in a mine near Cripple Creek.

LATER—Christison, the cattle thief and murderer, together with Sweeny, were arrested in Dobe park, on Cameron's ranch, three miles from Salida, while asleep in a loft. Armstrong and the mulatto, Smith,

Leadville Daily Herald, January 29, 1884

V. Christison worked thirty acres, raising 620 bushels of oats and barley on twelve acres of ground. He raised 25,000 pounds of potatoes on two acres, and put up twelve tons of native hay.

Salida Mail, December 8, 1891

HOWARD, January 18.—W. B. Jones has sold his ranch on Howard creek to E. V. Christison.

Salida Mail, January 20, 1893

Plead Guilty.

Last Saturday Ernest Christison, who has been lying in jail at Buena Vista since his recapture, under four indictments for cattle stealing, was allowed to withdraw his plea of not guilty and plead guilty to the same. Sentence is suspended for a time and from what we can learn may never be passed. It is believed an understanding has been reached by which Christison will give all the information he may have regarding the members and movements of the Chaffee county gang, so that cattle stealing can be entirely broken up for the present at least, in return for which he will not be sentenced but will have his liberty during good behavior. By this means it may once more become safe to run cattle in Chaffee county and the range will again be occupied. The range is a desirable one and will not long be wanting for cattle once the owners are assured they will be safe. Probably the indictments brought against Christison in this county will be quashed.

The Fairplay Flume, May 22, 1884

Jesse Huffman Stingley

Although uninvolved in the story of his uncle, Baxter, Jesse Huffman Stingley often confuses researchers. Multiple genealogy reports co-mingle Jesse Huffman Stingley with his cousins, Martin Jesse Stingley and Jesse Hooper Stingley. Born in 1869 to Baxter's brother, Absalom, Jessie eventually migrated to Colorado. He married Mary A. Murnane in 1900 in Boulder. One article, written after his tragic death, reports that he lived in Salida, but this is probably the result of an honest mistake, confusing him with his cousin, Jesse Hooper.

Jessie Huffman Stingley was murdered in 1912 while working as a railroad detective investigating a boxcar theft ring. Three men beat Jesse to death, and his body was discovered days later. All three murderers were convicted.

Adding to the tragedy, his wife died weeks later of a broken heart, leaving two children under ten.

Denver.—His head beaten to a pulp with a crowbar, with three bullets in the brain and a bullet in the back, the dead body of Jesse H. Stingley, a detective, was found in a clump of weeds about 300 feet from the Denver, Northwestern & Pacific railroad station at Utah Junction, three miles north of Denver, in Adams county The body was discovered by C. H Vinton, a fellow detective, who had been sent out to hunt for Stingley when the latter failed to report for duty or return to his home.

The Middle Park Times, November 1, 1912

Mrs. Jesse H. Stingley, the wife of the detective murdered by Frank L. Smith and W. P. Code at Utah Junction six weeks ago, is dying. Bereft of her reason as a result of worry over her husband's death and stricken with paralysis, she lies at death's door at St. Joseph's hospital in Denver.

The Salida Record, December 6, 1912

Frank Reed

No one ever found a trace of the murderer. Frank Reed simply disappeared.

Marshal Baxter Stingley

Stingley's grave, at Cleora Cemetery, is no longer visible. Either the site was covered up when the State expanded Highway 50, cutting across part of the burial ground, or the location was forgotten. There are over 200 graves at this graveyard with missing or deteriorated, unreadable headstones.

Jesse Hooper Stingley

Of all those involved in this story, Jesse Hooper Stingley seems to have led the saddest life.

Jesse sold his interest in the Kansas butcher shop in late 1885 and returned to Colorado, two years after the murder of his uncle. Jesse bounced between mining towns until he came back to Salida in 1893 but remained unsettled and constantly on the move until his death.

Rheumatism.

Jesse Stingley having sold his interest in the Main street butcher shop to his partner, Wm. Fultz, has, with his family, gone to Colorado.

Independent-Journal, December 41, 1885

In 1900, he divorced his wife, Nettie Maria Cameron. The divorce must have been amicable because Jesse partnered with his ex-father-in-law, Thomas Cameron, to open a meat market in 1897. The joint venture lasted one year before Jesse left to chase a gold claim. The two men opened another meat market in 1912.

In 1908, Jesse Hooper remarried, this time to Nettie Wilder of Colorado Springs. He promised her they would move to Seattle, Washington. They did not. Two years later, Nettie went to Seattle 'for health reasons.' The couple later divorced, and in 1915, Jesse married Effie Hanagan and remained wed until his death.

Jesse never seemed to find contentment or peace, constantly bouncing between wives, locations, and jobs. He died in 1928 in Gallup, New Mexico, where he worked as a contractor.

Following are articles documenting Jesse Hooper Stingley's many stops and life changes.

J. H. Stingley, with his family and household goods, left Monday morning last for Salida, where they will reside.— Wason Miner.

Salida Mail, quoting Creede Wason Miner, August 22, 1893

Ground is broken on M. W. Alexanander's place for a house to be erected for Mr. Stingley who will farm a part of Mr. Alexander's ranch next season.

Salida Mail, October 24, 1893

Thomas Cameron and wife visited their daughters, Mrs. Bowers and Mrs. Stingley, at Howard, on Saturday last.

Salida Mail, September 7, 1894

Jesse Stingley has secured a position in a meat market at Florence, to which place he went last night.

Salida Mail, December 14, 1894

Freeman Bros. have had their hay baler in active operation here the past week baling hay at the ranches of Messrs. Stout, Stingley and Longaker. They are shipping a car load of hay to Leadville to-day.

Salida Mail, February 8, 1895

Jesse Stingley, a former resident of Howard is running an express wagon at Cripple Creek.

Salida Mail, March 6, 1896

In the northern part of the section and east of the property owned by the Colorado Coal & Iron company, gold values predominate and several good prospects have been opened, particularly by Harrington and Stingley, each of whom have lead assays from $50 to $116 from a depth of ten feet. In the southern part and east of the Colorado Coal & Iron company's property considerable excitement has been occasioned within the last week over the discovery of bodies of ore running in lead and silver. An assay of ore taken at a depth of five feet gave 31 per cent lead, 3.8 ounces silver and a trace of gold. The formation is lime quartzite and porphyry. The ore is found in contact veins carrying large bodies of the mineral, which is crystalized lead and galena with some brown hematite iron running in gold.

Chaffee County Republican, June 2, 1897

Opening and Closing Hours.

Cameron, Stingley & Co. wish to announce that their market will be open to customers from 5 30 a. m. until 8 p. m. independent of the opening and closing of other markets.

Salida Mail, August 17, 1897

Mining Notes.

Stingley et al, of Salida, are arranging to continue development of the Hallie S., located in the Mahoa section, in the northwest quarter (of section 30. The shaft is 38 feet down and assays run from $1.80 to $120 in gold.

The Whitehorn News, May 6, 1898

Notice of Dissolution.

Notice is hereby given that the firm of Cameron & Stingley, doing business in Salida, was by mutual consent dissolved on May 20, 1898, J. H. Stingley retiring.

All bills will be collected and obligations paid by T. B. Cameron, who will continue the business. All parties indebted to the firm of Cameron & Stingley will please call and settle.

T. B. CAMERON.
J. H. STINGLEY.

Salida Mail, May 24, 1898

Cheatum and Stingley are now putting in regular time working in the mine, and if the work continues they are liable to follow in the footsteps of our friend Evans and become permanent fixtures here.

The Aspen Times, August 11, 1898

Jesse Stingley has returned from Telluride where he has for several months been employed in a market. He will remain permanently in Salida with his family, but has not definitely decided what business he will follow.

If you go to Leadville be sure you get there. We know a man who tried to get there the other evening but the brakeman forgot to call "change cars at Malta" and he landed in Minturn to wait for the next train back. However he saw several Salida boys who are located at Minturn and all are doing well. Jess Stingley is night operator and Alex. Wilson is round house foreman. J. H. Gilroy is running freight between Minturn and Grand Junction. Will and Tom Haley are doing a prosperous business and Walter Crawford is employed by them. Minturn is a nice place but it is not so big as Leadville and the next time that fellow starts to the cloud city he is going to tie a string to the brakeman.

Jesse Stingley yesterday hauled five tons of 60 per cent copper ore from Henry Silt's mine on Badger creek to Howard from which place it will be shipped. Mr. Stingly says he believes the mine is a bonanza.

Salida Mail, June 30, 1899

Jesse Stingley, who is now operator at Tennessee Pass come down this morning.

Salida Mail, August 22, 1900

company will operate in Leadville.

Jesse Stingley, who has been for some time located at Minturn as an operator for the Rio Grande, has decided to quit the key and return to mining. He is in Idaho Springs where he and Arthur Roller have some mutual interests.

The Whitehorn News, February 15, 1901

Mr. and Mrs. J. H. Stingley, formerly of Red Cliff, Colo., are at the home of Mr. and Mrs. Arthur H. Roller. Mr Stingley has accepted the position of foreman on the Shafter mine, and when a suitable house can be procured, will locate here.

Idaho Springs Siftings, February 21, 1901

Jesse Stingley was in Denver the latter part of last week, returning Sunday accompanied by his two children who had been for some time in the Good Shepherd school. The children were not satisfied with their surroundings and it was thought best to have them at home with their father.

Salida Record, February 14, 1902

The Opera Block Meat Market will open Saturday morning,
J. Stingley. Prop.

Rocky Ford Enterprise, February 8, 1907

STINGLEY-WILDER

Sunday, March 1, was surely a day favored by Cupid for the consummation of his ardent efforts to combine for life the victims of his archery. Amongst the couples who on that day were joined in matrimony was J. H. Stingley, former proprietor of the Opera Block Market, and Mrs. Nettie Wilder of Colorado Springs. The ceremony was performed at the home of Walter Cheek by Rev. S. C. Green. Immediately after the ceremony the happy pair left for Seattle, where they will reside.

Rocky Ford Enterprise, March 6, 1908

A thoroughly up to-date and first class market is to be opened on East First street about Saturday. The cooler for the meats will cost $600 and is on the way from Waterloo, Iowa, being the most expensive pattern made. The butcher shop is the largest in town and the meats handled will be only of the very best, selected by experienced men. Schmidt & Stingley, well known around Salida and Monarch for twenty years or more. Everything in connection with the market is to be first class and the location, the Hauke building, will be convenient to all parts of the city. These gentlemen are bound to do their share of the business because of their knowl edge of the butcher business and their courteous way of treating their customers or any others with whom they come in contact. They are universal favorites with all who know them.

Salida Mail, November 24, 1908

Mrs. J. H. Stingley, wife of the genial proprietor of the People's Market, has been forced to take a several month's sojourn in Seattle on account of her health. She left for that city yesterday and will be missed by her many friends.

Salida Mail, March 16, 1909

NOTICE

Salida, Colo., March 7, 1910.
Having purchased of J. H. Stingley his entire interests cattle, stocks and book account in the "Peoples Market," located at 136 East First street Salida, Colo., known as the firm of Stingley and Schmidt I hereby agree to settle all accounts and pay all bills of Stingley and Schmidt, People's Market, and release J. H. Stingley from all further responsibility.

Signed this 7th day of March, 1910.
KARL SCHMIDT.
J. H. STINGLEY.

Salida Mail, March 15, 1910

Cameron, Stingley & Co., have opened a meat market at Gessert's old stand.

Salida Record, August 12, 1912

Mr. J. H. Stingley and daughter, Mrs. C. H. Thompson left Saturday for Denver, to attend the funeral of Mr. Stingley's nephew and name sake, J. H. Stingley, the De Lue Agency Operative, who was found murdered in the Colorado and Southern yards at Utah Junction, Friday Oct. 25th.

Salida Mail, October 29, 1912

Surrounded by many weeping friends, the body of Mrs. Jesse F. Stingley of Denver was lowered into a grave besides that of her husband, the murdered detective.

The Wray Rattler, December 12, 1912

J. H. Stingley left for Gallup, New Mexico, Saturday night, where he has accepted a position.

Salida Record, February 21, 1913

APPENDIX

Baxter Stingley's Family Tree

March 24, 1817
Father Jesse Bush was born in Ohio

1839
Brother Absalom was born in Indiana

1841
Sister Charlotte was born in Indiana

1843
Sister Clora was born in Indiana

1845
Benjamin Baxter Stingley was born in Missouri

July 15, 1851
Sister Mary Alice was born in Indiana when Baxter was six years old

February 8, 1854
Sister Rachel Olive was born in Lafayette, Indiana when Baxter was nine years old

March 7, 1856
Sister Martha Martisha was born in Maryville, Missouri, when Baxter was 11 years old

1857
Stepbrother Jesse Hooper Hughes born

August 1859
Brother Martin Jesse was born in Missouri when Baxter was 14 years old

1860
Sister Clora died

1861
Sister Charlotte was born in 1861 when Baxter was 16 years old

April 5, 1862
Sister Octavio was born in Iowa when Baxter was 17 years old

January 10, 1868
Mother Christina died in Winterset, Iowa, at the age of 49 when Baxter was 23 years old

October 15, 1869
Father Jesse remarried to Susannah Boicourt in Independence, Missouri

1870
Jessee Hooper Hughes, and two siblings, lived in the Stingley household after their mother married Jesse Bush Stingley

May 18, 1870
Half-sister Lillie May was born in Kansas City, Missouri, when Baxter was 25 years old.

March 4, 1873
Half-brother Samuel Harrison was born in Kansas City, Missouri, when Baxter was 28 years old

1878
Sister Mary Alice died

April 5, 1882
Jesse Hooper Stingley married Nettie Maria Cameron in Salida

October 28, 1883
Benjamin Baxter Stingley was murdered in Salida, Colorado, at the age of 38

1887
Father Jesse died at the age of 70

1900
Sister Octavia died

1910
Brother Absalom died

1912
Jesse Huffman Stingley murdered in Junction City, Utah

1923
Sister Charlotte died

1928
Jesse Hooper Stingley died in Gallup, New Mexico, at the age of 61

1937
Half-brother Samuel Harrison died

1942
Sister Rachel Olive died
Half-sister Lillie May died

1946
Sister Martha Martisa died

Benjamin Baxter Stingley Personal Timeline

1845
Benjamin Baxter Stingley was born in Missouri

1850
Lived in Lauramie, Indiana

1860
Lived in Nodaway, Missouri

1867 (estimated)
At least by this date, lived in Denver, Colorado

July 1, 1872
Baxter received a homestead patent from U.S. Land Office in Denver

1875
Participated in the Lake County War as a member of the *Committee of Safety*

1880
Lived in Alpine, Colorado, operating a saloon

Moved to Cleora, Colorado, to open a saloon

June, 1880
Benjamin moved to Salida, Colorado, and opened Stingley & Company, a saloon, with Charlie A. Hawkins

Built a home near Second Street and F Street in Salida

October 1880
Appointed to the Challenging Committee to ensure the legitimacy of elections

1881
Sold interest in Stingley & Company to Charlies A. Hawkins and move to Poncha Springs, Colorado, to open a saloon

August 1881
Lived in Junction City, Colorado

October 1881
Appointed Deputy Marshal of Salida, Colorado

November 1881
Appointed Marshal of Salida, Colorado

April 7, 1882
Brother Jesse Hooper Stingley married Nettie Maria Cameron in Salida, Colorado

November 1882
Elected Constable of Salida, Colorado

May 30, 1883
Shot in the chest and groin at Bender's Hotel in Salida, Colorado by Thomas Ninemeyer and his gang

August 15, 1883
Stood against local ranchers and ranchers from outside of Salida, Colorado, when they arrive in town for a trial, accused of stealing cattle from Lauren Edwin Watkins

August 1883
Returned from a business trip in Texas and swore revenge against those who murdered his friend Lauren Edwin Watkins in Canon City, Colorado

September 1883
Backs down in a standoff with Frank Reed and Bent Jamison while attempting to serve a warrant when Frank Reed gets the drop on him with a rifle

October 28, 1883
Murdered at Arbour Dance Hall in Salida, Colorado by Frank Reed. Baxter was 38

Jesse Hooper Stingley Personal Timeline

1880
Lived in Salida, Colorado, working as a butcher and sausage maker.

1882
Married Nettie Maria Cameron

March, 1883
Returned to Kansas and opened a meat market

December, 1885
Returned to Colorado

August 1893
Moved to Howard, Colorado, to farm

December 1894
Moved to Florence, Colorado, to work at a meat market

February 1895
Ranched in Howard, Colorado

March 1896
Operated an express wagon in Cripple Creek, Colorado

June 1897
Operated a mine in Chaffee County, Colorado

August 1897
Opened Cameron, Stingley & Company, a meat market, with Thomas Cameron

May 1898
Sold interest in a meat market to return to mining

Late 1898
Lived in Telluride, Colorado, working in a market

January 1899
Lived in Minturn, Colorado, working as a night operator for the railroad

June 1899
Mined at Badger Creek

March 1900
Divorced wife, Nettie Maria

August 1900
Railroad operator on Tennessee Pass

February 1901
Lived in Idaho Springs, Colorado, working as a foreman on the Shafter Mine

February 1902
Lived in Salida with his two children, whom he retrieved from Denver (ostensibly, they were living with their mother)

February 1907
Opened meat marketing in Rocky Ford, Colorado

March 1908
Married Nettie Wilder

November 1908
Opened Schmidt & Stingley People's Market in Salida

March 1909
Wife Nettie left for Seattle for health reasons (they is no further record of her, but he later remarries)

March 1910
Sold all his cattle and interest in People's Market

February 1913
Left Salida for Gallup, New Mexico

1928
Died while working as a contractor in Gallup, New Mexico

Thomas Cameron Family Tree

Thomas Cameron (1830-1897)
& wife Elizabeth Boon Cameron (1834-1902)

James Bruce Cameron, son (1856-1940)

Robert Rowland Cameron, son (1857-1934)

Tamer Eliza Cameron, daughter (1861-1913)

Nettie Maria Cameron, daughter (1863-1944)—married to Jessie
Stingley (1882-1900)

Nancy Isabel Cameron, daughter (1865-1924)

Mollie Emily Cameron, daughter (1868-1936)

Truesdale Boon Cameron, son (1869-1954)

Hattie Estella Cameron, daughter (1875-1969)

Hugh Marion Cameron (1877-1895)

REFERENCES

A History of Chafee County—Buena Vista Heritage
Ancestry.com
Buena Vista Democrat
Carbonate Chronicle
Chalk Creek to the Past, Don Smith
Chattanooga Daily Times
Chicago Tribune
Daily Republican
Denver Land Office Records, 1862-1908
Denver Tribune
Deseret News
Down With Your Dust, Ruby G. Williamson
Dunkirk Evening Observer
Freeborn County Standard
Freemont Weekly News
Fremont Tri-Weekly Tribune
Grand Valley Star
Gunnison Review-Press
Heart of the Rockies—A History of the Salida Area, Kim Swift
Idaho Springs Siftings
Independent-Journal
Jackson County Banner
Las Animas Leader
Leadville Daily Herald
Library of Congress
Middlebury Register
Muscatine Weekly Journal
Ottawa Weekly Republic
Over Trails of Yesterday, The Hermit of Arborville

Quad-City Times
Reno Gazette-Journal
Rocky Ford Enterprise
Saguache Advance
Salida Mail
Salida Museum
Salida Record
Salida Regional Library
Salida, Colorado, 1880-1886, David J. Ham
Silver World
Sioux City Journal
St. Joseph Gazette
Standard
The Aspen Daily Times
The Aspen Times
The Aspen Weekly Times
The Avalanche-Echo
The Bourbon News
The Brooklyn Union
The Butte Miner
The Canon City Record
The Chaffee County Democrat
The Chaffee County Republican
The Chaffee County Times
The Charisma of Chalk Creek, Stella Hosmer Bailey
The Charlotte Observer
The Colorado Daily Chieftain
The Daily Chronicle
The Delta Chief
The Denver Tribune
The Des Moines Register
The Fairplay Flume
The Independent
The Indianapolis News
The Inter Ocean
The Journal Times
The Larimer County Independent
The Los Angeles Times
The Middle Park Times
The Mountain Mail
The New Mexican Review
The New York Times

The News and Observer
The News Journal
The People's Press
The Record-Union
The Republican Chronicle
The Rocky Mountain News
The Saint Paul Globe
The Salida Daily News
The Salida Record
The San Francisco Examiner
The Seattle Post-Intelligencer
The Sentinel
The State Journal
The Times-Picayune
The Whitehorn News
The Wilmington Morning Star
The Wray Rattler
The York Daily
U.S. City Directories
U.S. Find A Grave Index
U.S. General Land Office Records, 1796-1907
United States Census records
United States Officer Down Memorials, 1791-2014
Wason Miner

ABOUT THE AUTHOR

Steve is a historian and owner of Salida Walking Tours and Buena Vista Walking Tours.

He is the author of the 'Salida Sam' historical book series and writes/produces *A Salida Moment in History*, the 2019 Colorado Broadcasters Association Best Regularly Scheduled Program. He also writes/produces *A Buena Vista History Flashback*. Steve is a commissioner on the Salida Historic Preservation Commission.

For many years, he traveled full-time, living out of a Jeep and a tent, collecting experiences, stories, and friends. In addition to living in a dozen states in the U.S., Steve resided in Aruba, Canada, China, Indonesia, Malaysia, Mexico, the Philippines, Singapore, St. Thomas, and Thailand.

When not indulging his inner history-nerd, he is usually exploring the mountains of Colorado with Gina (a 2005 Jeep Wrangler) and his four-legged best friend, Rez (a 2018 Red Heeler/Basenji mix).

Email: StevenTChapman970@gmail.com

Walking Tours

Salida & Buena Vista

See historic Salida through the eyes of a local on this intimate small-group walking tour. Experience Salida's wild west past, history, culture, and architecture with a professional guide. Be captivated by fascinating tales of Salida's exciting, and sometimes violent, history. Visitors and residents alike come away with hidden secrets.

Costumed guides lead this intimate, small-group walking tour. Be entranced by fascinating tales of Salida's remarkable history. Visitors and residents alike are amazed to learn the many hidden secrets of Colorado's largest National Historic District.

www.SalidaWalkingTours.com

Also by Steven T. Chapman

THE 'SALIDA SAM' HISTORICAL BOOK SERIES

Each book covers two years of Salida history, detailing nearly every fact, with rarely seen photographs and maps.

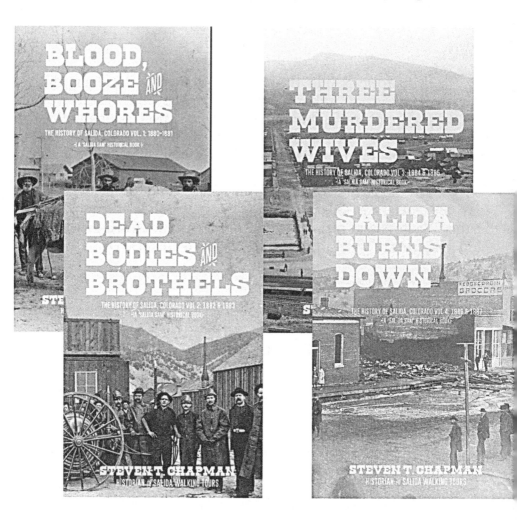

www.SalidaWalkingTours.com/shop

Tune In...

A Salida Moment in Time
2019 Colorado Broadcasters Association
Best Regularly Scheduled Program

&

A Buena Vista History Flashback

Written & produced by Steve Chapman

Heard throughout the day in Salida on
Eagle Country 104.1 FM, Hippie Radio 97.5 FM,
and The Peak, 92.3 FM
Listen on www.HeartOfTheRockiesRadio.com

Made in the USA
Monee, IL
12 August 2023

40908440R00108